HOME WINEMAKING THE RIGHT WAY

Kenneth Hawkins

RIGHT WAY

Contents

DEDICATION

To Eddie, with many thanks for the
inspiration,
I raise my glass.

1

INTRODUCTION

Noah was the first man to plant the vine
'He drank of the wine and was drunk' – Genesis
– the story goes that he lived to the age of 350 years.

There was a time in my life when I did not make wine – it was a long while ago, but I can still remember it vaguely. Before I was married, my father 'dabbled' in the hobby, but neither his efforts, nor the results, interested me greatly, and although I have always been fond of good living, circumstances at that time only allowed for the tasting of a commercial wine on very rare occasions. My attitude to country wines was rather condescending – it was a substitute, and I was a perfectionist. In any case, the hobby was not active enough for someone who was fond of almost any form of physical exercise. However, time goes by, as it is apt to do, and this, together with a rather serious illness, left me without a hobby, and feeling very sorry for myself.

To the clergyman who introduced me to winemaking, I shall be forever indebted, for he did much more than give me an absorbing hobby. He gave me a renewed interest in life at a time when it was really needed, and apart from that hobby, the introduction to a host of new friends through a winemaking club, and a comradeship there that I have rarely found elsewhere. (See Chapter 11 for the advantages to be gained from belonging to a winemaking club.)

As a result of my experience, my main concern has always been to try to help the beginner and in doing so to *keep it simple*. This is for two reasons: firstly as our hobby *can* be simple if that is what we want of it; and secondly, due to the fact that I am no chemist anyway. I may comment on many of the modern sophisticated items now available to us, but my strong advice to those about to take up this fascinating hobby is, do not initially buy a lot of expensive equipment – learn your craft first, let your enthusiasm build up, and gradually add those little extras as you feel the need for them.

Though I hope to cover most aspects of the craft during the course of the book, the 'Purists' may well be disappointed, for it will contain my personal experiences, some of which may not follow the accepted pattern. I do not apologise for this, since my results have brought a fair success over the past few years, and in any case, I have found so many conflicting statements in some of the books that are now available, that I am sure that I am not alone in writing from my own experience.

Although this book is not intended to be a textbook for the experienced winemaker, I feel that many of the recipes, and their lay-out, may be of interest to all those who enjoy participation in the craft.

Winemaking has probably become one of the most popular craft hobbies and has many attractions for those who appreciate the odd glass of wine, either with a meal, or simply on a social occasion. In these days of high taxation, our own wines are relatively cheap to make, and the hobby gives a feeling of achievement in the same way as the ability to cook an excellent meal. But unlike cooking, it is a hobby that can occupy the individual for two hours a month or twenty, according to the time and space available, and the degree of enthusiasm that the hobby has created. (Before we go any further, it must be pointed out that the law in Great Britain allows us to make any amount of wine *for our own consumption*, but we must not sell a drop, or allow it to be sold for profit, as no duty has been paid. Neither are we allowed to distil.)

The declared definition of wine is an alcoholic beverage made from the fermented juice of the grape, fermented in the country of origin – all of which may be quite acceptable to the countries whose climates permit the growing of grapes in sufficient quantities to enable them to fulfil their needs, and possibly to export, but it is hardly satisfactory for countries such as the U.K. Nowadays the utilisation of other fruits etc. has become such an interesting craft that there are thousands of 'amateurs' (and I use this word with trepidation, for many of them know a great deal both about the ingredients used, and the commercial wines of the world) who are quite capable of making an alcoholic drink which is at least the equal of the middle range commercial product. Of course there are many whose efforts leave much to be desired – producing alcoholic drinks, perhaps, but for one reason or another, not up to the standard.

I hope that this book will enable anyone, even those who are new to the craft, to reach an acceptable level. By this I do not mean that all wines should become copies of the commercial product, but simply that we use them as a comparison for quality, as obviously a commercial wine must have a market value, and this becomes the best standard the amateur winemaker has to set against his or her own efforts.

As you will see, our home-made wines can be produced from an infinite variety of ingredients – flowers, fruit, grain, honey, leaves and vegetables – but experience will probably show that the best results will usually be obtained from a recipe that includes an element of fruit in it, otherwise there may be a tendency for a lack of vinosity in the finished wine. By all means experiment with other available ingredients later on, but it is better for the beginner to learn his or her craft first, before going into the intricacies of blending ingredients without the aid of a proven recipe.

Home-made wines have been made in this country for hundreds of years, using fruits from the hedgerows, flowers, vegetables etc., with honey as the sweetening agent. The first set-back to home winemaking came when the Bordeaux area fell under British rule, and for many years imports of French wines were enjoyed by the more prosperous, leaving the making of country wines to the poorer classes. Later, when those territories were lost, wines were imported from Portugal, with whom Britain had a trade treaty. In the eighteenth century the quantity of sugar imported caused the price to fall within reach of the working man, and from then onwards the use of honey declined, and gradually malt beers began to take over. As a nation, the making of wines declined, and it was indeed fortunate for us that our forebears kept, and handed down, many of the old recipes, for they are still the basis of some of our country wines today.

Many of us have heard stories of how strong the home-made wines were 'in Grandma's day'. Don't believe a word of it. Present-day yeast strains and expertise are infinitely superior. It was simply that in those days the cheapness of spirits made it possible for home-made wines to be fortified with brandy. Those days are gone, and if our wines are to be as strong, we must bring this about by our own efforts, such as the control of sugar, and the use of the appropriate yeast culture, in order to keep down costs.

These last thirty years have seen significant advances in the craft. New strains of yeast have become available, fining and filtering methods have been greatly improved, and with these better facilities, and the knowledge of how the alcoholic content can be controlled, we are now able to produce what we know as 'Purpose Wines', i.e. aperitifs, table wines, dessert wines, sparkling wines, and even liqueurs (or wines for before, during and after the meal) and I will go into these in detail in Chapter 5.

Finally, never be afraid to ask advice from an experienced winemaker – I have always found them to be most helpful.

The origins of winemaking

Before going on to the equipment which will be needed, I would like to include a little story of the very early days of winemaking, interesting, although I cannot guarantee its accuracy. However, I would not quarrel with the description of the wine, for taken in moderation, wine can be an aid to the digestion, is full of vitamins, and in fact is one of God's great gifts to mankind.

Jamshed, first king of the Persians, and according to legend, a grandson of Noah, became an old man and lost his teeth, but he so liked the grape that he ordered his servants to press a large quantity so that he could enjoy the juice. As he wished to have the juice throughout the winter months, the stock was to be kept in great containers. After a few days, however, he noticed that the juice had changed its appearance and tasted bitter. He was very sad, and thought that the juice had gone bad and was poisonous. In order that no one should inadvertently drink it, he ordered that it should be placed in the cellar, the door locked, and on the cellar door, the word 'Poisonous' printed.

Soon afterwards a favourite slave had a terrible headache which caused her many sleepless nights, and she felt that she wanted to die. Finally she thought of the poisonous juice, and crept down to the cellar. After sampling the juice, she began to feel quite happy and could no longer feel the pain. The more she drank, the better she felt, until she finally fell asleep in the cellar. In the meantime her absence had been noticed, and a search for her began. After a while she was found, but she continued to sleep for two days and two nights – it is said mainly from the exhaustion of those sleepless nights. She finally woke to find the king present and very anxious about her. The headache was gone and she felt in the best of health. The king was so overjoyed that he, too, decided to sample the 'poison'. He also became happy and carefree, and gave the drink the name of the 'Medicine of Kings'.

2

EQUIPMENT

What do we need in the way of equipment? At the outset, keep it simple. Don't buy a lot of sophisticated equipment until you are sure that you really need it. The following is a list of what is either essential, or at least advisable.

A two gallon (nine litre) bucket, preferably of good quality, rigid, white, non-toxic plastic. (Avoid the use of earthenware, which may be lead-based; enamel, which if crazed may taint a wine by contact with metal; and also any brass or copper containers.)

A cover for the bucket, either a plastic lid, or a sheet of plastic which can be tied on to exclude air.

A large sieve or piece of muslin.

A large funnel, preferably large enough for the sieve to fit into it.

A large wooden or plastic spoon.

Glass jars or demijohns – the quantity will depend on the individual, but always keep one empty jar for use in syphoning off the wine.

Non-toxic plastic containers may be used for short-term purposes, but not for storage, and do not use a plastic container which has previously been used for vinegar.

Airlocks, airlock bungs and either corks or rubber bungs for each jar – I prefer the rubber ones as they are easier to sterilise.

A length of rubber or plastic tubing for syphoning off the wine.

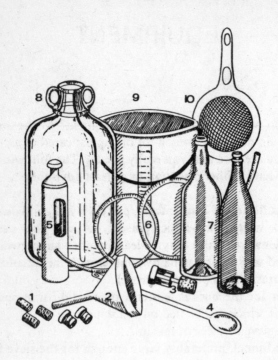

Fig. 1 Some Equipment.

1. Corks (straight and competition-type).
2. Plastic funnel.
3. Airlock and cork.
4. Large plastic or wooden spoon:
5. A corker or 'flogger'.
6. Rubber or plastic syphon tube.
7. Punted bottles for red and white wines.
8. Glass demijohn or fermentation jar.
9. 2 gallon (9 litre) plastic bucket.
10. Sieve.

A hydrometer and jar (more about this in Chapter 7).
A corker for use when bottling.
A supply of citric acid, tartaric acid and straight corks.
A quantity of bottles, preferably punted (i.e. not flat-based).
Labels.
A bottle brush.
A thermometer.

Sterilising The Equipment

It will be noticed that there is no mention of any agent for sterilising the equipment in the above list. Cleanliness is possibly the most important aspect of winemaking, and yet one which can so easily be overlooked. It is not only that the equipment should appear to be clean, it should be *chemically* clean. Hot water and a brush are all very well, but a quick swill will not necessarily kill all bacteria. The use of either Campden tablets or a sodium metabisulphite solution is essential if the ingredients are to be given the best possible start.

If Campden tablets are to be used, dissolve two, together with a saltspoonful of citric acid, in one pint ($\frac{1}{2}$ litre) of water, and thoroughly cleanse all equipment to be used. If made in larger quantities and kept in a tightly corked jar, this solution may be used and re-used over a prolonged period before it begins to lose its efficiency.

Campden tablets are in fact sodium metabisulphite, and whilst they are convenient to handle, and obviously the quantity of the chemical is easy to assess when in tablet form, it is cheaper to make up a sterilising solution using sodium metabisulphite in powder form: 5 oz (140g) to the gallon (4.5 litres) or $\frac{1}{2}$ oz (14g) to the pint ($\frac{1}{2}$ litre). One word of warning: do *not* breathe the sulphur dioxide fumes given off when the sodium metabisulphate or Campden tablets are mixed with water.

Having prepared the solution, place some in jars, bottles and funnel, using a stiff brush to assist in cleaning off. The airlocks and syphoning tube should also be soaked for a few minutes. Perhaps the most important of all is the plastic bucket into which the must will be placed. Inevitably these buckets become scratched in time, and thereby provide an ideal hiding place for bacteria. Leave the solution in the bucket for a few minutes, and then rinse it out with hot water before use. Once the bucket is as germ-free as possible, care must be taken to ensure that bacteria is not re-introduced by the ingredients themselves – to be entirely free is very difficult, but wash the fruit, particularly dried fruit which is coated with a preservative when packed. When the ingredients and water are all in the bucket, add one Campden tablet and leave overnight. After 24 hours the yeast starter may be added, and should soon provide the protection of alcohol which will kill off any remaining bacteria cells before any lasting damage can be done.

Beware of friends who insist that they never use more than hot water – they may appear to be safe for some considerable time, but there could be a day of reckoning, and down the drain goes a gallon of wine and a lot of effort.

Having given a list of equipment needed, perhaps I should explain a few of the terms that are found in winemaking.

Airlock or Fermentation Lock
There are many types, in glass or in plastic, and although some types look complicated and highly professional, the simplest little plastic airlock is quite adequate. As the name suggests, the airlock protects the fermenting ingredients by excluding the air, which could cause oxidation, and gives protection from the vinegar or fruit fly, which is one of our greatest enemies, whilst still allowing the carbon dioxide gas

to escape into the atmosphere. The airlock should always be kept half-filled with water.

Body
The fullness of a wine – the best illustration is the comparison between a light table wine and a heavy port. Table wines are generally light- to medium-bodied, whereas ports and dessert wines are full-bodied.

Cap
This is the fermenting head of the liquor which contains quantities of the ingredients raised to the surface by the action of the yeast.

Carbon Dioxide
A colourless, odourless gas, produced by the yeast during the fermentation process, which must be allowed to escape into the atmosphere. If retained in the jar or bottle, the gas will build up pressure which will ultimately burst the container. Carbon dioxide is heavier than air, and will therefore form a protective blanket over the fermenting must in the early stages.

Dry
A term given to a wine from which the sugar has fermented out completely.

Enzymes
These are organic catalysts produced by the living yeast cells. There are many different types in our wines, each having one specific job to do. It should be remembered that as wine is a living thing, changes will be taking place throughout its life.

Fermentation on the Pulp
The first heavy or aerobic fermentation (see page 23).

Filtering

A method of extracting particles of solids and dead yeast cells from a wine which has not cleared naturally. Filtering should be used as a last resort, for it does, on occasions, affect the flavour of a wine, particularly if it is a light, delicate, table wine.

Fining

Preferable to filtering, but even so, do let Nature try to clear a wine first. There are several types of fining agents, and sachets are often issued with many of the kits now on the market – this is simply to allow the beginner to produce a drinkable wine at an earlier date, but with a little patience any well-balanced wine should clear by itself, and the slightly longer wait will be amply repaid by the production of a better and more matured wine. I shall be going further into this in later chapters.

Gravity (s.g.)

Short for specific gravity, the measurement used to check the degree of sweetness of a wine. If taken at the beginning of the ferment with the hydrometer, and again at the end, a calculation can be made which will give the alcoholic content of the finished wine. The method will be shown later when we consider the use of the hydrometer in Chapter 7.

Lees

The yeast and solid deposit formed during fermentation.

Liquor

The liquid containing sugar and other ingredients which will eventually become wine when the yeast has completed its work.

Must
The pulp or basic ingredients from which the wine is made.

Nutrient or Nutrient Salts
A yeast food.

Oxidation
The effect caused in a wine by too much contact with the air. Though acceptable in a sherry wine, it is objectionable in a light table wine. The only possible cure for this is to make a further batch of the same wine, and when it is in full ferment, add the oxidised wine, and continue the ferment in the usual way. It is essential that the quantity of oxidised wine added does not exceed the second batch in volume, and I would not even advise this cure if the original wine was badly oxidised.

Purpose Wines
Wines that are made for the occasion of a meal. These consist of aperitifs (for before the meal), table wines (drunk during the meal) and dessert wines (sweeter, heavier wines which are consumed after the meal). This, of course, means we must learn to control the alcoholic content far more accurately, and this again brings us into contact with the hydrometer, a most useful instrument in winemaking, which I will go into fully in Chapter 7.

Racking
Syphoning off the wine from the lees.

Stable
The condition of the wine when all fermentation has ceased, i.e. when all the yeast cells have been inhibited by the alcohol produced.

Sulphiting the Must

Adding a crushed or soluble Campden tablet the day before the yeast is added, ensuring freedom from bacteria.

Second Run

Using the basic materials for a second time in order to produce a lighter table wine. It is usually necessary to add acid and either raisins or sultanas in order to ensure vinosity, and if undertaken, I would suggest a short fermentation on the pulp.

Starter Bottle

Using a starter bottle is the best method of starting a fermentation. A starter is usually prepared at least 24 hours before preparation of the must, or 48 hours if using a liquid yeast.

INGREDIENTS

12 fl oz (340ml) water
3 tsp sugar
¼ tsp citric acid
Juice of an orange
Sachet of a suitable wine yeast
   or tsp of general purpose wine yeast
Pinch of nutrient salts

PROCEDURE

Boil the water and then allow it to cool to about 75°F (24°C). Place it in a small bottle, add the sugar, citric acid and the juice of the orange. Mix in the wine yeast and add the nutrient salts. Plug the bottle with cotton wool, and keep the starter in a warm place. When the starter is well under way, stir it into the must.

Vinosity
This is a term used to identify the wine-like nature of an alcoholic drink.

3

FERMENTATION

Fermentation is in reality a complete series of processes, and is controlled by enzymes which are produced by the yeast cells themselves. Simplified, and as far as we are concerned, it is a process by which the yeast breaks down sugar into its constituent parts of glucose and fructose, and gradually converts them into alcohol and carbon dioxide in almost equal proportions, together with several smaller bi-products, of which glycerol (2%) and succinic acid (1% of the alcoholic content) are the most important. (Glycerol adds body to a wine, and succinic acid assists to promote ester production, which in turn, gives the vinous character we need.)

A sound fermentation of the must is of great importance to us, and it should begin as soon as possible after the ingredients are in the bucket and the effect of the Campden tablet has worn off. It is for this reason that I would always advocate the use of a starter bottle (see page 20), as it minimises the 'time-lag' when the must is most vulnerable to the growth of bacteria; for in creating the ideal temperature for the yeast to work, we have also produced the best conditions for the growth of bacteria.

To do its work, the yeast must have the right environment – that is, a temperature of 65–75°F (18–24°C) in a sweetened liquid with some acidity. The starter will quickly produce a blanket of carbon dioxide over the fermenting must, and this will help to protect it from bacteria as long as the bucket is covered. The must should be stirred at least once a day, firstly to break up the 'cap' of solids forced to the surface by the yeast, secondly to obtain the best possible extraction, and thirdly in order to introduce a little oxygen into the must. For the best results, an even temperature of about 70°F (21°C) should be maintained throughout the fermentation.

The first heavy ferment is known as the 'aerobic' ferment (or open to some air), and this will continue for four or five days. As soon as it subsides, the must should be strained by using a sieve or piece of muslin, and the liquor placed in a demijohn under airlock, making sure that the jar is topped up to within $1\frac{1}{2}$ in (38mm) of the cork with water. The fermentation will then continue more slowly in what is known as the 'anaerobic' fermentation.

The speed of a complete ferment will vary considerably from one wine to another, and it is not always the fastest fermenting yeast that provides the best wine. An early start and a steady ferment are the keys. A ferment will proceed until the yeast has either used up all the sugar, in which case it is a dry wine, or alternatively, until the amount of alcohol produced has inhibited the yeast cells, which have died, leaving a sweet wine. This, then gives us a most important piece of knowledge – the amount of sugar controls the dryness of the finished wine, remembering, of course, that some fruits have a greater amount of natural sugar than others, and this natural sugar must be taken into account when assessing the requirements for any particular wine.

You will know the fermentation is complete when the bubbles stop bubbling through the airlock into the outside air, but make sure that fermentation has not stopped for some other reason (see page 64 on stuck ferments). Those using a hydrometer should refer to page 51 for the recognised finishing gravities.

4 BALANCE

In order to obtain the best possible fermentation, it is essential that the balance of ingredients is right. The grape is the only fruit to have this balance, which is, acid, flavour, sugar, tannin, water and yeast. Therefore our recipes must contain all these ingredients as nearly as possible in the same proportion if we are to produce a quality wine (see Charts 1 and 2). As none of our fruits is complete in itself, it is not unusual for more than one to be blended in order to obtain this balance. Another way to achieve the right balance is to add grape concentrate, but I suggest only a small quantity. This also improves the vinosity of the wine.

Acid
Because many of our fruits and other winemaking ingredients are short of acid to a greater or lesser degree, some addition will probably be necessary. This acid may be added in several ways – it may be by means of a lemon, or grapes, or just a dry acid. I believe that the dry acid method is best, for it is the only simple way to control the *quantity*.

Chart 1
Table for selecting ingredients for balanced red wines

Using the chart below you can compare the amounts of aroma, acid, tannin and flavour contained in different fruits etc. with the ideal amounts contained in black grapes.

FRUIT	AROMA	ACID	TANNIN	FLAVOUR
Black Grapes*	**XX**	**XXX**	**XXX**	**XX**
Bilberries (fresh)	XX	X	XX	XXXX
Blackberries	XXX	XXXX	XX	XXXX
Blackcurrants	X	XXX	XX	X to XX
Black Plums	XX	XX	X	XX
Cherries (eating)	XX	XX	X	XX
Cherries (morello)	XXX	XXX	X	XXXX
Damsons	XX	XXXX	X	XXX
Elderberries	X	X	XXXX	XX
Loganberries	XXXX	XXX	X	XXX
Mulberries	X	XXX	XX	XX
Raspberries	XXXX	XX	X	XXX
Redcurrants	XX	XXX	X	X
Red Grape Concentrate	X to XX	XX	X to XX	X
Sloes	XX	XXX	XXXX	XXX
Strawberries	XX	X	X	X to XX

* 100% juice
Others: 4 lb (1.8kg) per gallon.

Chart 2
Table for selecting ingredients for balanced white wines

Using the chart below you can compare the amounts of aroma, acid, tannin and flavour contained in different fruits etc. with the ideal amounts contained in white grapes.

FRUIT ETC	AROMA	ACID	TANNIN	FLAVOUR
White Grapes*	XX	XXX	X to XX	X to XX
Apples (cooking)*	XX	XX to XXX	XX	XX
Apples (crab)	XXX	XXX	XXX	XXX
Apples (dessert)*	XXX	XX	XX	XXX
Apricots (fresh)	XXX	XX	X	XXX
Gooseberries (cooking)	X	XXX	X	X
Gooseberries (dessert)	XX	XX	X	XX
Oranges	XX	XX to XXX	0 to X	X to XXX
Peaches (fresh)	XXX	XX	X	XXX
Pears (eating)*	XX	X to XX	X to XX	XX
Pears (perry)*	XX	XXX	XXX	XXX
Quince (orchard)	XXX	XXX	XXX	XXX
Rhubarb	0 to X	XXX	XX	0 to X
White Currants	XX	XXX	X	XX
White Grape Concentrate	X	XX to XXX	0 to X	X to XX
Yellow Plums	XX	XX	XX	XX
Cowslip†	XX	0	0	XX
Dandelion†	X	0	0	XX
Elderflower†	XXX	0	0	X
Rose Petal†	XXX	0	0	X

*100% juice; †1 quart of flowers to the gallon; others 4 lb (1.8kg) per gallon.

After all, if the recipe calls for the addition of one lemon, is it a large one? small one? extra dry? or extra juicy? No one knows how much acid has really been added, and even if the result gives a perfect balance, there is very little chance of repeating it.

The acid found in the lemon is citric, and this is probably the most widely used. However, it is not the only acid to be found in the ingredients suitable for winemaking. Tartaric acid is found in grapes; malic acid in apples and most of the stone fruits, and also to a lesser degree in grapes. It follows that all these acids may also be used in powder form, and indeed, I believe that a mixture of all three will produce the best results. 50% tartaric, 30% malic, and 20% citric would seem to be an excellent blend, bearing in mind the acid content of the fruits we are using. Chart 3 shows the different types of acid found in fruits and flowers etc. (Remember, however that where a fruit is shown to have more than one acid, the number of parts shown on the chart is only a ratio, and does not mean that because a fruit has ten parts it is more acid than one with less parts – an example of this is the strawberry, which although low in acid, has a nine to one proportion of citric to malic.)

Tannin
When we come to tannin, we find that some of our ingredients are so bland that its addition may also be advisable (see Charts 1 and 2). Tannin is the additive that gives wine that 'bite' – without it a wine would appear to be flat and uninteresting (winemakers call it bland). Most red wines have sufficient, the tannin being in the skins of the fruit, but many white wines may need a little – not more than a level saltspoonful of grape tannin powder to the gallon or alternatively a few drops of a liquid tannin solution.

Apart from the fact that tannin helps to bring a wine to

Chart 3
Table showing the different types of acid found in various ingredients

INGREDIENT	TYPE OF ACID				
	CITRIC	MALIC	TARTARIC	SUCCINIC	OXALIC
Apples		✓			
Apricots	3	1			
Bananas	1	1			
Beetroot	✓				
Blackberries	1	2		*	
Blackcurrants	✓	*			*
Carrots	1	2			
Cherries		✓			
Damsons		✓			
Elderberries	✓				
Figs	✓				
Gooseberries		✓			
Grapes		✓	✓		
Grapefruit	✓				
Greengages		✓			
Lemons	✓				
Loganberries	✓				
Oranges	✓				
Parsnips	1	3			
Peaches	1	1			
Pears	2	1			
Pineapples	7	1			
Plums		✓			
Prunes		✓			
Raisins			✓		
Raspberries	✓				
Redcurrants	✓	*		*	
Rhubarb	5	16			2
Sloes		✓			
Strawberries	9	1			
Sultanas			✓		
Tangerines	✓				

For Gooseberries, Grapes, Grapefruit: { The proportion varies according to variety.

✓ indicates the presence of a particular acid.

* indicates that the fruit only contains trace elements of the acid. Where a fruit has more than one acid the numbers show the proportion of each acid to the others e.g. apricots have a 3 to 1 proportion of citric to malic acid.

'life', it is also useful as an aid to clarification. In some wines, particularly those in which the elderberry predominates, the tannin content may be unacceptably high, but if this is the case, do not despair, time will result in much of the tannin dropping through, and many a rough young wine has turned out to be first-class after a more prolonged maturation period.

Yeasts

Yeasts are now available to us which greatly encourage the production of good wines. For the beginners perhaps a general purpose yeast may be sufficient, but for those who wish to make wines to type, we now have ranges of yeasts, cultivated from the grapes grown and used in the production of most of the well-known area wines. Given the right ingredients, there is no reason why we should not produce fair copies of many commercial wines (see Charts 4(a) and 4(b)). These special yeasts are available in liquid or granule form, but whichever is chosen, a yeast starter will give the best results, as it will minimise the 'lag period' before the yeast has been able to produce that blanket of carbon dioxide necessary to minimise the possibility of bacterial infection.

Do not be misled into believing any recipe for a 'no yeast' wine. There is no such thing – without yeast there can be no ferment. In these recipes, it simply means that the wild yeasts to be found on the skins of the fruits have been allowed to take over, and the result of this will be a wine that is low in alcohol, and will in all probability be left with off flavours. All fruits should be thoroughly washed before use, and when the wild yeasts have been cleared, then the wine yeast may be added.

Chart 4(a)
Showing suggested yeasts for use with ingredients mentioned

INGREDIENTS	HOCK	SAUTERNES	TOKAY	PORT	MADEIRA	BURGUNDY	CHABLIS	SHERRY	BORDEAUX	CHAMPAGNE	ALL-PURPOSE
Apple	✓	✓					✓				✓
Apricot (dried)	✓								✓		✓
Apricot (fresh)	✓	✓	✓								✓
Banana		✓	✓				✓				✓
Barley		✓							✓		✓
Beetroot					✓						✓
Bilberry				✓		✓					✓
Blackberry			✓	✓		✓			✓		✓
Blackcurrant				✓		✓			✓		✓
Bullace					✓	✓			✓		✓
Carrot		✓						✓			✓
Cherry		✓	✓	✓	✓	✓			✓		✓
Cowslip	✓	✓								✓	✓
Crab apple		✓								✓	✓
Damson				✓		✓			✓		✓
Dandelion	✓									✓	✓
Date					✓				✓		✓
Elderberry			✓	✓		✓			✓		✓
Elderflower										✓	✓

Chart 4(b)
Showing suggested yeasts for use with ingredients mentioned

INGREDIENTS	HOCK	SAUTERNES	TOKAY	PORT	MADEIRA	BURGUNDY	CHABLIS	SHERRY	BORDEAUX	CHAMPAGNE	ALL-PURPOSE
Fig			✓		✓			✓			✓
Gooseberry	✓	✓	✓		✓		✓	✓		✓	✓
Grapefruit	✓		✓						✓		✓
Loganberry				✓		✓			✓		✓
Mixed Dried Fruit			✓		✓			✓			✓
Mulberry			✓						✓		✓
Orange	✓	✓			✓		✓	✓			✓
Parsley			✓					✓			✓
Parsnip		✓					✓	✓			✓
Peach	✓	✓	✓					✓			✓
Pea-pod			✓					✓	✓		✓
Pear	✓	✓						✓		✓	✓
Pineapple			✓						✓		✓
Plum	✓	✓	✓			✓	✓		✓		✓
Potato		✓									✓
Prune			✓		✓		✓	✓			✓
Raisin	✓		✓		✓		✓	✓			✓
Redcurrant									✓	✓	✓
Rhubarb	✓					✓				✓	✓
Rice			✓						✓		✓
Rose Petal									✓		✓
Wheat			✓						✓		✓

Sugar

We have already touched on the sugar content. Never overdo the sugar in the initial must. It can always be added during the ferment if necessary, but once in, if the yeast is unable to cope, a sweet wine is bound to result. Even if making a sweet dessert wine, it is of considerable advantage if the sugar is added in stages. This enables the yeast to work much better and helps to produce a wine with a stronger alcoholic content. Additional sugar may be added dry, though this does create some problem in dissolving it, or it may be added as invert sugar. This can be made up in batches and added to the fermenting wine as required. It is quite simple to make, and the recipe is as follows:

Ingredients
2 lb (900g) granulated sugar
Pint (½ litre) cold water
½ tsp citric acid

Procedure
Place the sugar, half a pint (285ml) of the water and the citric acid into a saucepan. Bring to the boil, stirring regularly, and simmer for 20 to 25 minutes until it begins to turn to a light golden brown colour. Then add the rest of the water, stir in and leave to cool. This will produce two pints of invert sugar. So the addition of a quarter of a pint of invert sugar is equal to the addition of a quarter of a pound of sugar.

Flavour and Water
In our balanced wines there remain two other constituent

parts, and these must be inter-related: the fruit (or other ingredient), and the water content. Quantity and treatment of the solids depend entirely on the type used, and at first it might be assumed that the water content should equal the volume of wine produced, i.e. normally eight pints (four and a half litres). However, juices and grape concentrate form part of the eight pints, and allowance for these should be made out of the water to be added, otherwise there may be a tendency for the wine to be thin.

To a certain extent the body of the wine may be helped by the length of time that the solids are left in the fermenting must, but there is a danger that a long aerobic fermentation may extract not only the flavours we want, but also some of the 'nasties' caused by the deterioration of the ingredients or the autolisation of the dead yeast cells. For this reason it is suggested that a period of five days fermentation on solids should be the maximum – in fact, many experienced winemakers will give a maximum of three days for a table wine, or simply liquidise the must, strain off and ferment solely on the juice. This will certainly give a quicker fermentation, with reduced tannin content in the case of red wines, but there must be a certain loss of body as well, or alternatively an increase in the quantity of fruit used.

Vitamin B$_1$ and Epsom Salts

Two minor ingredients which will be found in the recipes in this book may appear to be a little unusual to those about to start the hobby. Firstly, the suggested inclusion of vitamin B$_1$ tablets – not essential, but they do aid the yeast, and thereby the fermentation process. Secondly, the addition of a small quantity of Epsom salts (magnesium sulphate) – again by no means essential, but where included, Epsom salts have been found to be beneficial in hardening the water where the supply tends to be rather soft. In hard water areas there is no need for their inclusion.

5   TYPES OF WINE

Mead and its History

As everyone knows, this is a pleasant alcoholic drink made by fermenting honey and water with yeast. Of all the crafts of our ancestors, mead-making must rank amongst the oldest. Cave paintings of Stone Age man show the collection of honey from bee colonies, and as it was only necessary to add water to the honey to obtain a ferment from wild yeasts, it seems inevitable that alcohol was discovered this way.

In early Greek civilisation Bacchus was the God of Mead long before becoming the God of Wine. Mead was also offered to the goddess Aphrodite by ladies of good breeding to ensure a plentiful supply of lovers. Well-matured mead was kept for a twice a year celebration.

Later the Moors knew mead as a love stimulant, and in fact the deeper one goes into the origins of mead, the more one is convinced, not only that it is the oldest drink (known in some form in every ancient civilisation) but also that it always seemed to be connected with, or allegedly have powers in, the field of 'amour'. It is common knowledge that the word 'honeymoon' was derived from the practice of drinking honey-wine during the month-long celebrations which followed better class weddings.

Though mead, in its simplest form, consisted solely of honey, water and wild yeast, in its more sophisticated form it had various additives, and was known under a variety of lovely names: Melomel, Hippocras, Cyser, Pyment and Metheglin, containing fruit juices, grape and herbs, apple juice, grape, and various herbs respectively. It is from these old recipes that we have gradually developed our country wines.

Although we are inclined to call any honey drink mead, apart from wine mead, there was also a beer or ale mead. In fact the Anglo Saxon word for mead was 'alu', which is close enough to ale to be thought to be a derivation of the word. The British were never a wine-drinking nation to the same extent as the French or Italians, and in the days when only honey was available as a sweetening agent, beer and ale gradually became the staple drinks. In medieval times, the brewer of bad ale might be put into the 'cucking stool'. This was a chair in which the culprit was made to sit, either at his own door, or in some public place, where the population could see and mock to their hearts' content. Up to the eighteenth century the birth of a child was celebrated in the new father's house, with the fathers of twins sitting at the top table, the fathers of one or more children at the second, and the childless and bachelors at the third (there would be no table-cloth on the third table). This occasion was known as 'sops and ale' and was a great occasion for toasting, eating and drinking. There was certainly an ale-like drink up to the time of the Napoleonic Wars, since trouble occurred in the British Army when the alcoholic strength of the mead supplied to the troops was reduced from 6% to 4%. This was ale strength, and the mead was in fact made with hops and brewers' yeast.

Social Wines

The present day definition would probably be a wine with plenty of flavour, too strong in alcohol for a table wine, but not strong enough in either flavour or alcohol for a dessert wine. These wines can be sweet or dry according to taste. In fact, they are classic examples of some of the old country wines, which were made from whatever fruits, vegetables, etc. were available at the time, providing a wine that was suitable for drinking with friends in the evenings. There will be several examples of these social wines in the recipes following, and indeed they form a very useful introduction into winemaking for the beginner.

Purpose Wines

With this group of wines we are endeavouring to copy the *type* of wine, and not necessarily a particular commercial wine belonging to the group. We must select our ingredients with greater care with these wines, for it is no use trying to make a dessert wine, for instance with redcurrants. There is simply not the colour, body or flavour for such a wine. The ingredients must be capable of producing the type of wine we require, and it is hoped that the reader will find the notes against each recipe a help in this respect.

Aperitifs – The definition of these wines is that they should be suitable for drinking before a meal, and should cleanse and waken the palate in preparation for the food to come.

They may be sweet or dry according to type, and although they do not have to be fino sherries or sweet vermouths, this is an indication of what we need. Suitable ingredients for a dry aperitif are parsnips or the citrus fruits, all of which need the addition of sultanas or grape concentrate to give the necessary vinosity. In alcoholic strength they should be at least 16% by volume, and in many instances these wines are lightly fortified, either with vodka or Polish spirit. Most wines of this type are medium to heavy in body, and unless the winemaker is aiming at a sherry, they are often improved by the inclusion of a very small quantity of herbs or quinine. The yeasts used should be capable of working in a high alcoholic wine: Madeira or Tokay yeasts are suitable or, of course, Gervin 4 or sherry yeast if a dry or sweet sherry is the target.

Table Wines
Remember the purpose of these wines is to enhance food, not to dominate it, therefore avoid strong flavours.

Red wines – Usually light to medium in body, and mostly with a delicate but *good* bouquet – this is very important. These table wines should be dry unless rosé (which should come within the range of 998 to 1004 s.g. on the hydrometer – see Chapter 7). Alcoholic content will rarely exceed 12% by volume, representing a starting gravity of about 1078. Suitable yeasts for the red wines are Beaujolais for the light-bodied wines; Gervin 2, Burgundy or Bordeaux for the medium. Blackberries, elderberries, damsons and red grape concentrate are all suitable ingredients, also blackcurrants in small quantities.

White wines – Mainly light-bodied, with the exception of white Burgundy in the dry wines and Sauternes in the sweet. Alcoholic content is similar to the red wines, except in the case of a Sauternes type, which should be both heavier in body and in alcohol. Flower and leaf wines would fall into this category, though it must be remembered that all these wines will need to have bananas, sultanas or grape concentrate included in the recipe, otherwise they will be thin and without character. Yeasts suitable for the group of table wines are for the light-bodied, Graves, Hock, Chablis, Champagne, etc. and for the medium wines, Gervin 1, Bordeaux or Sauternes.

Dessert Wines

These wines are sweet and full-bodied, and should be fairly strong in flavour. The alcoholic content should be at least 16% by volume, more if possible. In most cases it will be necessary to include at least four pounds of fresh fruit per gallon, and add bananas, raisins or sultanas for increased body. Acidity will be higher than in the other groups, though this will be masked by the sweetness.

After Dinner Wines

This group will include port types, Oloroso sherries, Madeira, etc. and must be full-bodied and even stronger in flavour. They are heavy in alcohol, up to 18% if possible, and are sweet and often fortified. Yeasts suitable are Madeira, Tokay, Tarragona or Gervin 6.

Liqueurs

Commercial liqueurs can be split into two types – liqueurs and eau de vie.

The first should be made basically from spirits and a flavouring matter such as herbs, fruit, vegetables or flowers added prior to distillation, or alternatively the herbs, fruits etc. are macerated in the spirit for a varying period according to the strength of the additive. In either case the sugar is added later.

The second, eau de vie, are pure distillates made from fruit or vegetable wines, and should not contain any additional flavouring, just sugar to sweeten – examples of these are Framboise (raspberry), Kirsch (cherry), Calvados (apple).

The names of many of these liqueurs have been registered, and we are unable to use them, but there are several firms who are marketing liqueur essences which are very close to commercial types, and it is possible for us to make very acceptable liqueurs with the minimum of effort.

In selecting the wine to be used as a base, do not use your best. The most important thing to remember is that your wine must accept the flavour of the essence, not fight it, and you should therefore look for a mild flavour, but one strong in alcohol. Use a red wine for cherry brandy of course, but a golden wine is suitable for most liqueurs.

For home consumption it is not necessary for you to make the liqueur up to the strength of the commercial equivalent, but this is obviously a matter for the individual. For those who do, I must say that there is one very important piece of knowledge you must have, and that is the working of the 'Pearson Square'. For the purpose of this, let us say that we are endeavouring to make the equivalent of a crème de menthe, set out the details as follows:

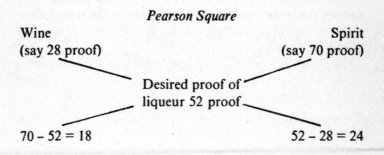

Pearson Square

Wine
(say 28 proof)

Spirit
(say 70 proof)

Desired proof of
liqueur 52 proof

70 – 52 = 18

52 – 28 = 24

The ratio is therefore 18 parts of wine to 24 parts of spirit
or 3 parts of wine to 4 parts of spirit.

The ingredients for a half bottle would therefore be:

    4½ fl oz (128ml) wine
    6 fl oz (170ml) spirit (vodka or Polish spirit)
    Invert or caster sugar to taste
        (quantity dependent on the sweetness of the wine)
    1½ tsp essence
    Glycerol to thicken the liqueur

Mix thoroughly. This will be drinkable at once, but it does improve with keeping, particularly as the glycerol does not blend easily.

It is not necessary, however, to copy a commercial liqueur. Why not blend one from your own favourite fruit, herbs, etc.? There are endless possibilities in our country wines – what about the richness of a loganberry or mulberry liqueur? Pineapple? Mint? There is no need to make up a large quantity, just a few fluid ounces to enable you to assess the value of the experiment.

The other method of making a liqueur is probably known to most people: that of steeping fruit in a spirit, adding sugar, and letting Nature do the rest. Such drinks as sloe gin, apricot gin, damson gin, are old favourites, but are certainly not as cheap to make as those made by the first method, and cannot really be considered a challenge to the winemaker.

6   THE PALATE

So now we know what can be done, given the right ingredients and the correct treatment. The majority of beginners will undoubtedly start by making country wines, and their progress will depend largely on the interest the craft creates for them. To make a real success of the hobby, however, there are two more aspects which should be mastered, and these can only be attained with experience.

Palate Training

The first is palate training, and here a knowledge of commercial wines can be of inestimable value. Why a commercial wine? Because it is at least a standard, in fact the only standard we really have, for the fact that the wine is made for sale means that it has a value, and to a certain extent its price gives an indication of quality. Nowadays many of us are only able to sample wines from the lower end of the market, but even so, do take any opportunity of tasting and comparing commercial wines with those produced at home. At first you may feel that your palate is not sufficiently developed to appreciate the finer points, but time will bring about a vast improvement, and this can be speeded up if you happen to be in contact with a group of fellow enthusiasts and can discuss the merits and faults with them.

First of all, then, what is the palate? It consists of three parts – the tongue, the throat and the nose. When we know the principles on which it works, we begin to know which part to use in order to recognise different factors. The golden rule is to try to ignore the obvious and look for the subtleties of flavour and bouquet which will make or mar the wine to be tasted. Sweetness will do much to mask a fault in a wine, but our palates will need to be able to detect the fault if our winemaking is to improve. I always advise anyone to taste the must just prior to the addition of the yeast starter. At first this may not mean very much to the beginner, but gradually it will enable him or her to assess the right acidity and potential flavour.

The tongue is able to detect the presence of bitterness, acid, sugar and salt – B.A.S.S. The top surface of the tongue is covered by up to 9,000 taste buds, each consisting of about 15 taste cells rather like the segments of an orange. Certain areas of the tongue are more perceptive in picking out different flavours:

Front of tongue	Sugar
Left and right outer edges	Salt
Back and back half of sides	Acid
Back of tongue	Bitterness.

The tongue, then, should give us a lot of information about the wine we are tasting. But not only have we to recognise these different flavours, but also be able to assess the degree of each.

To obtain the best results it is advisable to have a wine glass which is narrow at the top in order to concentrate the bouquet. A sherry glass would do, but better still a tulip glass or copita, which is the type used by wine judges. The glass should be filled to its widest part, and a good mouthful of wine taken. Whilst the wine is at the front of the mouth and tongue, the degree of sweetness will be most noticeable. The wine should then be allowed to flow round the mouth (it is called 'chewing it') and as it passes the sides of the tongue the acidity will become more apparent. Salt is something which would hardly be found in a wine anyway. As the wine reaches the back of the throat, any bitterness will become apparent, though if this is only very slight, it may only be noticeable when a little of the wine has been swallowed, and the bitterness then comes as a back flavour.

At the top of the nasal system is a region known as the olfactory region which senses a smell and transmits a message direct to the brain. It is not yet established how many types of smell the nose can identify, but obviously with training it is able to tell us what is good in a wine and what is bad. For instance, the 'nose' of a wine which has acetic acid in it and is turning to vinegar will be known before the taste-buds ever come into contact with it. When inhaling a wine, take a deep breath, note the inviting (or otherwise) nature of the bouquet, for this impression is a most important one. The nose will also give an indication of the degree of sweetness, vinous quality and balance, though this can on occasions be a little misleading, particularly if the wine is young and yeasty. Constant practice will, however, soon enable you to concentrate on the less obvious aspects of a wine, and give invaluable assistance towards the production of quality wines.

A Wine Memory
Whilst this training of the palate is very important, I believe

that the second aspect is equally so, that is, for a winemaker at any level to train him or herself to build up a 'wine memory'. It would be useless to taste commercial wines in an endeavour to copy them, or even to use them as a guide, if the lessons learned from that tasting were not remembered and stored away in the memory. Again, this is a long-term project, but once it is mastered it will be of the greatest assistance in blending your own wines in order to bring about the best possible results. Don't worry if progress seems to be slow, a Master Winemaker or National Judge was a beginner once, and possibly years have passed before they have attained these accolades in the craft.

7

USE OF HYDROMETER

I realise that many of those about to take up the hobby have no intention of going to the extra trouble of controlling the alcoholic content, but for those who do, and would ultimately wish to emulate commercial types, the hydrometer and jar become virtual necessities.

A hydrometer is very simple to use. Although it really measures the density of a liquid, it does give us a reasonably accurate indication of the degree of sweetness of a finished wine, and, if used at the beginning and end of the fermentation, an indication of the alcoholic content of that wine. The hydrometer has a bulbous weighted end, and is a tube which is graduated along its length, normally from 990 at the top to 1170 at the bottom. These numbers refer to the specific gravity, and if the hydrometer is placed in a tall, narrow, glass jar which has been filled with water, it will float at a level that gives a reading of 1000. If alcohol is added, a lower reading will result, as alcohol has a lower density than water; but if sugar is added, the reading will be higher, as sugar is of greater density, and the amount of sugar will be indicated. Therefore, if a reading is taken from the must in the bucket just prior to fermentation, that reading will give the total sugar content, i.e. the combination of the natural sugar from the ingredients and the sugar that has been added.

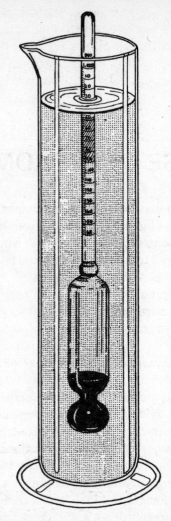

Fig. 2   Hydrometer and Trial Jar.
(floating in water it gives a reading of 1000)

To obtain an accurate reading, the reading should be taken
when the temperature of the liquid is at 60°F (15.5°C) and
the hydrometer should be given a spin as it is placed in the jar

in order to throw off any air bubbles which may be attached. Having taken the first reading, the same procedure should be adopted at the end of the ferment. By taking the second figure from the first, the drop in specific gravity is obtained. Divide this figure by 7.36 to find the percentage of the alcohol by volume. Then, if you multiply this percentage of alcohol by volume by 7 and divide by 4, your final answer will give you the proof spirit of the wine.

The following is an example of how it works:

First reading	1086	Specific gravity
Final reading	998	Specific gravity
	———	
Drop	88	

$88 \div 7.36 = 11.96\%$ alcohol by volume

$11.96 \times 7/4 = 20.93$ proof spirit

This, then, is how we learn to assess the amount of alcohol in our wines, and we are now in a position to make table wines, aperitifs, dessert wines, etc. as well as to ensure that the wines finish with the correct amount of sugar content for their type.

The beginner will notice that the recipes in this book sometimes advise that part only of the sugar content or sugar-containing ingredients should be added during the fermentation. Obviously, in these cases the first reading will not give the total sugar content. We get over this problem of assessing the gravity quite simply by taking one hydrometer reading before the additional ingredient is added, another

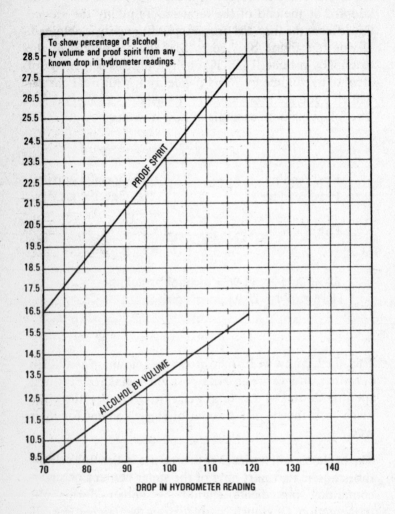

DROP IN HYDROMETER READING

immediately afterwards, and adding the increase to the original gravity of the must.

Commercial wines do not always show the alcoholic content on the label. Even when they do, it can vary quite a lot. An indication of the range of content is as follows:

Table wines	— between 10% and 12.5% by volume, except in Sauternes, which may be as high as 14%; German types and rosés are usually amongst the lower percentages.
Aperitifs	— between 12.5% and 16% according to type.
Dessert wines	— 16% and above.

In all instances, it is best if these wines are allowed to ferment to dryness, and be left to mature in this state until required, for a dry wine always matures better than a sweet one, particularly in bulk. Once the wine has matured, a stabilising tablet (available from winemaking shops) could be added before sweetening the wine. (The stabilising tablet should avoid the possibility of any re-ferment.) After adding a stabilising tablet, leave the wine in the demijohn for a few days before bottling.

The recognised finishing gravities are:

For dry wines	— under 1000 s.g. (if possible down to 990 s.g.).
For medium wines	— 1000 s.g. to 1008 s.g.
For sweet wines	— above 1008 s.g. preferably above 1018 s.g. but if a Sauternes type, this could be as high as 1030 s.g. (though at this degree of sweetness, a little additional acid may well be required, otherwise the wine may tend to cloy).

8 RACKING, PROCESSING AND MATURING

Racking

Racking is the term used to describe the drawing off of the wine from the deposits of solids and yeast cells (known as the lees) which have accumulated at the base of the fermentation jar. If left, these solids will decompose. When a yeast cell is exhausted and dies, it sinks to the bottom of the jar, where a series of chemical reactions takes place, known as autolysis or self-destruction. Enzymes gradually turn the cell back to its basic constituents, which are released into the bulk of the wine. Some of these constituent parts are then used by the remaining yeast colony, but some are less desirable, and could impart an off flavour in the new wine. It follows, therefore, that the timing of the first racking is of primary importance, and will have a lasting effect on the quality of the wine.

Unfortunately it is very difficult to give fixed periods of time for racking as so much depends on the amount of debris that exists, and the speed of the ferment. A very rough guide would be – first racking after four weeks (always subject to the hydrometer reading indicating a dry wine, or at least a reading down to the degree of sweetness required in the finished wine), second racking after eight weeks, then as necessary at two monthly intervals until the wine is star-bright. Racking does help to clear a wine, but it does also reduce the yeast colony.

When drawing off the wine from the solids, place one end of the rubber tube halfway down the demijohn, suck the other end sharply in order to start the transfer of the wine and then place the tube at the bottom of the receiving demijohn.

Finally a warning – when racking a wine that is not yet stable, do ensure that it has minimum contact with the air. The syphoning tube should go deep into the receiving jar, not allowing the wine to splash. The action of racking will inevitably leave some oxygen in the wine, and an excess of oxygen is liable to cause oxidation, something which although acceptable to a certain extent in a sherry, would ruin a lighter table wine. At this first racking it is advisable to place one crushed Campden tablet to the gallon (four and a half litres) in the receiving demijohn as an insurance against possible oxidation. After subsequent rackings, there will probably be sufficient alcohol to counteract the risk, provided that the above racking instructions have been followed.

Processing And Maturing
Once our wine has ceased to ferment and has become stable,

this is not the end of our endeavours. If winemaking consisted solely of placing set quantities of ingredients in a bucket, and at given intervals, racking and bottling, then our hobby would not retain our interest for long. Louis Pasteur once wrote, 'There is never alcoholic fermentation without the continued life of cells already formed'. When we place the yeast in that bucket, we are helping to create a living thing, for the wine we shall ultimately drink will be changing constantly throughout its life. A complex series of chemical changes takes place, brought about firstly by esters – these are fragrant substances (responsible for the scents and flavours of plants and fruits) which are produced in wines by the action of organic acids on alcohol. Secondly by enzymes, which are lifeless substances produced by the living yeast cells.

Very few winemakers pay enough attention to the important subject of processing and maturing. To make wine, bottle it in about four months, and drink it very shortly afterwards, is all very well, and I do not doubt that your first few gallons will be consumed eagerly, but do try to put away at least one bottle from each batch and allow it to mature fully. As your palate becomes more discerning, you will begin to realise how much better your wines can become by allowing them to mature.

By processing I mean the attention given to the wine at each stage of preparation, particularly in the case of white wines, which should be racked regularly. With the addition of the one Campden tablet at the first racking, your wines will be secure against oxidation and darkening of colour – this is particularly necessary in the case of apples and pears. Always ensure that the fermentation jar is topped up to within 1½ inches (38mm) of the cork after racking, with water or if a light-bodied wine with another similar wine, that airlocks are kept half full (this is usually done with water, but glycerin is even better as it will not evaporate).

Also make sure that *all* your equipment is sterilised at all times.

Now for maturation, we are told that wines are best matured in barrels, but this is a luxury that very few of us possess. What is the alternative? Try to mature in bulk if at all possible, in glass jars, or even stoneware jars if you are sure that the glazing is sound. Up to two years for a strong wine, such as a dessert or port, less probably, nine to twelve months, for table wines. If you are fortunate enough to have a small barrel, keep it for red wines, for these will benefit most from it, but do varnish the exterior first in order to minimise the possibility of oxidation through the wood. If you are maturing in glass containers make sure the corks and bungs fit tightly to exclude the air. It is advisable to cover the jars in some way in order to exclude the light, which particularly with red wines, does affect the colour. A piece of newspaper wrapped round and held in place with a rubber band is quite adequate. Another way is to use brown-coloured demijohns for wines in store, but my objection to this is the difficulty in seeing through the glass in order to find out when a racking is necessary. In all instances a wine will benefit during the maturation period if it can be kept at a steady temperature of just under 60°F (15.5°C).

When bottling time comes round, syphon the wine from the demijohn. Always use a straight cork in preference to one with sloping slides, for if shrinkage does occur, the cork with the sloping sides is more likely to let in the air than one which is touching the neck of the bottle throughout its length. A tip, here, too: when forcing the cork into the neck of the bottle, have a piece of string (about 8 inches/20cm long) partially inside the bottle, but hanging outside. As soon as the cork is inserted, pull out the string, which will then release the air which has been compressed in the neck of the bottle by the insertion of the cork – failure to do this may result in the air pressure pushing the cork out again. There are several types of corking machines available to make the task easy. When the wine is bottled and corked, try to store the bottle at an angle – this will keep the cork moist and thus avoid shrinkage which could let in air.

It is important too, that the finished product should be made as attractive as possible to look at. Never bottle a wine before it is clear enough to drink, for there is nothing worse than being offered a drink from a bottle which has a layer of sediment on the bottom – it is unappetising to say the least, and think of the possibility of off flavours developing from the dead yeast cells which have accumulated in the bottle. Our bottles should be the correct ones for the type of wine they contain, that is, white for a white wine or coloured for a red, though this may be a little difficult at first until an adequate supply has been obtained. The bottles should be thoroughly sterilised before use, the wine star-bright, the cork well into the bottle, and the wine within half an inch (13mm) of the cork.

The labels should be attractive and neatly written, placed equidistant between the seams of the bottle, and sufficiently low that they lie flat – this is particularly important when using Burgundy-type sloping shoulder bottles. For the few extra minutes it takes, it is useful to add identity details such as the date of making, batch number, and whether sweet or dry. All this information will be of considerable use to you if you are keeping wines for any length of time. Some very decorative labels are available in shops selling winemaking equipment, though these can be quite expensive. If you intend to continue to make wine over a period of years, it is well worth considering the purchase of labels printed from a design you have made yourself. In the long term this can result in quite a substantial saving. The example shown gives the type of wine, batch number, hydrometer reading, alcoholic content, and the date made. In this case, I have a different colour label for each year, which enables me to see the age at a glance. For those who wish to go even further, there are such things as coloured cappings, and neck labels which indicate whether the wine is sweet or dry. All this may seem to be a little unnecessary, but I believe that it is not enough to know you are offering a good wine, it deserves to be *seen* to be at its best.

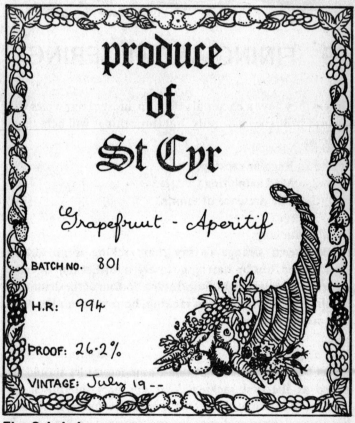

Fig. 3 Label.

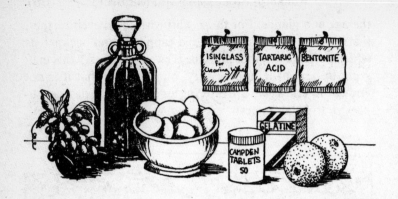

9 FINING AND FILTERING

Unless they have a bacterial infection, most of our wines will clear to brilliance naturally, but three things will help them to do so:

1. Regular racking.
2. Mild sulphiting.
3. The presence of tannin.

Regular Racking
It may seem strange to say that racking is an aid to clarification, but by watching closely, a further film of yeast and solid deposit will be found at the bottom of the demijohn within two or three days of racking, however clear the wine may seem to be.

Mild Sulphiting
It has been suggested that one Campden tablet should be added at the first racking. This not only minimises the possibility of oxidation, in that it disperses the oxygen which has entered the wine during the racking process, but again it is an aid to clarification.

The Presence of Tannin
The lack of tannin is one of the biggest causes of our winemaking difficulties. Adequate tannin not only gives a better ferment, and a better balance to the wine, but it is also an aid to clarification.

Fining

If we have a persistent haze in a wine, and we have assured ourselves that it is not a pectin or starch haze (see Chapter 10) we still have two methods of attempting to clear it – the first of which is known as fining. However, neither method is as good as Nature's own way, and I would advise its use only if really necessary. I know that many of the commercial kits now on the market provide a fining agent with all their wines, but this is simply to allow the less patient winemaker to obtain the finished product a few weeks earlier, and there is no doubt that some quality is sacrificed in doing this. Among fining agents are the following:

Isinglass – this is a pure type of gelatine, and a one ounce (28g) packet will fine 10 gallons (45 litres) of wine. Break down the fibres into a powder and dissolve in a cupful of water with a pinch of tartaric acid. This will set in a jelly. Add it to a jug full of wine, mix thoroughly, and add it to the bulk – it is no use adding the isinglass direct to the demijohn as it will not mix easily.

Gelatine – here, the active component of gluten plays a large part. This clearing agent has a positive charge, and should simply be dissolved in hot water, and stirred into the wine. Follow the instructions on the packet.

Albumen (egg white) – one egg will fine 10 gallons (45 litres). Whisk into part of the wine and add to the bulk.

Milk – which contains casein, is another fining agent, and this also has the effect of reducing the colour of the wine. For this purpose, prepare three small clear bottles with about 100cc of wine in each. To the first add ½cc of milk, to the second 1cc and to the third 1½cc. Shake them all thoroughly and leave for 36 hours. From the results you can select the colour you require. Then add the necessary quantity of milk to the bulk of the wine in that ratio.

Because of the difficulties in assessing the quantities required for so small an amount as one gallon (4½ litres), none of these methods is particularly popular with winemakers. Far safer is the use of one of the new proprietary brands of wine finings, the quantity to be used being shown on the containers.

It is most important in using any of these fining agents that the dosage is not exceeded, for this in itself can stabilise the haze, making it impossible for the wine to be cleared to brilliance.

There remains one other fining agent which has the advantage that its use entails no risk of overfining. It is known as *bentonite*, and is a clay which comes from America. One flat dessertspoonful in a cup of wine will be enough to fine a gallon of wine, but it must be mixed very thoroughly before it is added to the bulk. In liquid it tends to swell greatly, but if added to the wine in the correct consistency, it is quick in action and does an excellent job.

Filtering

If all else fails we can try filtering, but do use this method as a last resort, for it is inclined to take more than just the solids in suspension out of a wine. Many eminent winemakers insist that a wine so treated never recovers in full, and that occasionally the wine will have a slight taste of the filter medium. However, the last few years have seen great strides in the marketing of filtering aids. Up to that time an open funnel and filter paper were all we possessed, and this left the wine in constant contact with the air for lengthy periods with the obvious risk of oxidation. Recently, manufacturers have given considerable thought to the subject, and as a result we now have a number of filtering aids available to us. Most of these exclude the air completely during the filtering process, and are therefore relatively safe, though if using any of them it is advisable to allow the wine to recover before drinking.

10 WINE DISORDERS AND TREATMENT

In this book I do not propose to go into details of all the wine disorders that can arise, for many occur so rarely that the beginner would be extremely unfortunate to come into contact with them, particularly if the basic instructions on sterilisation have been strictly adhered to. However, there are one or two problems which are fairly common and may be encountered from time to time, and a little knowledge of these and the cure may be of assistance. There are two kinds of hazes which can occur in certain types of wine, both of which can be avoided at the outset if the winemaker has the knowledge.

A *pectin haze* is caused by a gelatinous substance in the fruit (what is good for jam-making often causes problems in winemaking) and the way to avoid this is to use a pectin-destroying enzyme in the must. The use of Pectinol, Pectolase, etc. in accordance with the manufacturer's instructions should prevent a pectin haze forming, but if the finished wine is still hazy, it can be tested for pectin by taking 3 fl oz (85ml) of methylated spirits, 1 fl oz (28ml) of wine, and stirring well. If, after a short while, jelly-like clots or strings begin to form, the haze is caused by the presence of pectin. The treatment is to add a teaspoonful of Pectolase to the wine, stir well, and keep it in a warm place for a few days, then rack, or filter if the haze does not clear.

The second is a *starch haze*, most noticeable in grain wines. To test for this, place a few drops of the wine on a white plate or tile, and add a few drops of iodine. If the mixture contains black spots or flecks, then starch is present. The treatment is to take $\frac{1}{2}$ oz (14g) of amylase and 3 fl oz (85ml) of water, place it in a bottle and leave for two hours, stirring and shaking it occasionally. Heat the wine to 170°F (76°C) and hold it at that level for twenty minutes. Cool to 100°F (38°C) and stir in the diluted enzyme. In one hour the reaction should be complete. Raise the temperature to 170°F (76°C) again, holding it at that temperature for ten minutes. After cooling, the haze should settle out, and the wine should be racked. All this is quite a lot of work, so to prevent a starch haze forming in the first place, it is far better to add amylase to the must at the rate of one teaspoonful to the gallon (4½ litres).

A third common fault found is *flatness or insipidness* in a wine. This is due to the lack of tannin in most cases, and can often be overcome by the addition of a few drops of a proprietary brand of liquid wine tannin solution (obtainable from any winemaking shop) or a cup of cold strong tea to the gallon (4½ litres). Either should be added when the wine is clear, but before maturing. The liquid tannin is preferable as the quantity of tannin is more easily controlled, and a cup of tea does weaken the alcoholic content to a certain extent.

Another of the problems which we sometimes have to face occurs during fermentation. It is known as *acetification*, and with this disorder the wine will gradually turn to vinegar. It is probably the most disastrous disorder, for although it can be stopped if noticed in the very early days, it is often not apparent until it has reached a level when nothing can be done. It can be caused in several ways, by bad storage, the presence of air, the vinegar or fruit fly, or even excessive heat. The last is not often considered, but it should be remembered that the heat in the cap of a must is at least five Fahrenheit degrees higher than the rest of the must. Excessive heat will kill the yeast, but still encourage the growth of bacteria known as Mycaderma Aceti, which will cause this acetification. Those with a keen sense of smell may notice if a wine has a slight tendency towards vinegar. If so, act at once – add two Campden tablets to the gallon (4½ litres) and leave for 24 hours. In the meantime, prepare a yeast starter in a bottle with the same type of yeast used in the original, and when the starter is fermenting, add a little of the wine (but never more than the amount in the starter bottle). Similarly, when this is fully fermenting, add the same amount of wine again, and continue to do this until the whole of the gallon is re-fermenting. Don't forget to sterilise the demijohn that held the infected wine very thoroughly, and also the cork and airlock.

Last, but certainly not least, is the problem that winemakers call a '*stuck ferment*'. This indicates that for some reason the yeast has failed to complete its work, and left us with an over-sweet wine. Stuck ferments are probably one of the more common faults, and may be caused by a number of things:

1 Acetification (which we have already looked into).

2 Excess sugar – this can suffocate the yeast. (But it is not a stuck ferment if the yeast has produced its normal alcoholic content and is still over-sweet. This is an error of judgment on our part in preparing the must.)

3 Carbon dioxide in the solution – airlocks should help avoid this, but a good shake up of the demijohn may be of assistance.

4 No yeast – usually caused by over racking, either too early or too often.

5 Insufficient air – this may seem strange, but $1\frac{1}{2}$ inches (38mm) should always be left between the level of the wine and the cork.

6 Lack of acid – wine may develop an off flavour, but if noticed in time, additional acid may help.

7 Presence of a preservative – this usually occurs when tinned or bottled fruit has been used. Check that tins are marked 'No preservatives', and in the case of dried fruit, ensure that it is thoroughly washed before use.

8 Temperature – either too high, in which case the yeast will have been killed, or too low, in which case the yeast has become dormant. Even an intense fluctuation of temperature can sometimes have the same effect.

9 Lack of nutrients – simply add a further half teaspoonful of nutrient salts.

I cannot close this chapter without giving the beginner some crumb of comfort: don't think that these problems make winemaking an extremely hazardous business – it is not, and with normal luck and adherence to the basic rules, it will only be on very rare occasions in times of trouble that there is any need to look up this section.

11   ENCOURAGEMENT

Those who have just set out on this wonderful hobby of ours
deserve all the encouragement winemakers can give them,
but apart from advice on a particular problem by an
individual, what can we do? What is the set-up throughout
the country? The craft of wine and beer making has made
great strides in the past 30 years – monthly journals are
available, in addition there are books on every aspect, and
from a very small beginning at Andover in 1953 has grown a
network of clubs, many of which are grouped into area
federations. Over all this we have the National Association
of Amateur Wine and Beermakers.

Some beginners have taken the first step themselves by
joining a wine club, but many hold back under the
impression that they will feel lost, out of their depth, and
amongst the 'professionals'. How wrong they are. Every
club has its quota of beginners, and many hold Beginners'
Classes from time to time. I feel sure that most people gain
more pleasure in learning the craft in the convivial

atmosphere of a wine club, where problems can be discussed with those who have already experienced them, and where there is a social life for the taking. Many club members are content simply to make the occasional gallon in the time-honoured way, and are unlikely to be influenced by competitions, or indeed anything that I may say, but if the newcomer is keen enough, it is possible to progress right up to the stage of becoming a National Judge. Most clubs will hold regular competitions, including Novices' Classes, and although they would obviously like a high percentage of members to take part, it is an accepted fact that many will not do so for one reason or another, and no one should feel bound to enter.

Many clubs are affiliated to their area federations, and it is usual for a federation to hold training classes for senior wine and beer makers, who, after passing written and practical examinations, and proving their ability by suitable competition results, may become Regional Judges. Some of the federations also have their own Masters' Guild, where experienced and qualified members meet to discuss some of the more technical aspects of the craft, and to carry out experimental work, the results of which can be taken back to the clubs. In addition, a federation will hold its own Annual Festival, in which all member clubs may compete, and this is usually followed by a social event in the evening.

Membership of the National Association is open to federations, clubs, and to individual members. The Association exists to further the interests and knowledge of the craft, and to hold an annual competition.

Finally, I must say a few words about that dedicated body, the National Guild of Judges. Membership is by a very strict examination, of course, but members of the Guild always seem available to judge at our festivals, to advise, and to give talks etc. I sometimes wonder how they manage to find time to make any wine or beers for themselves. Without the members of the Guild we would be unable to run these competitions and indeed the standard of our wine and beer making would soon deteriorate.

I have mentioned competitions, which of course exist at all levels, club, federation and national, and although it must be admitted that only a small percentage of members enter, there are many advantages to be gained by those who do. From Novices' Classes in a club competition onwards, there is the pride of achievement, the challenge of beating the existing champion, or simply of gaining points for one's club. Also, practical help is obtained from the advice willingly given by the judges, and by the comparison with other members' wines.

12 RECIPES

All the recipes are for one gallon (4½ litres) unless otherwise stated. In the recipes: tbsp = tablespoon; tsp = teaspoon; dsp = dessertspoon; pt = pint.

The indication of the type of wine against each recipe does not necessarily mean that the yeast will leave the degree of residual sugar associated with that type of wine when it has completed its work. It is simply that the author believes that each recipe will produce the wine at its best if it does contain that amount of sugar. This may well mean that sugar should be added once the wine is stable.

However, when sweetening a wine at the end of a ferment do make sure that the wine is really stable, for any dormant yeast cells can easily restart a ferment when sugar is added – the addition of one stabilising tablet (available from winemaking shops) per gallon should avoid any difficulty. (Of course, if a Campden tablet has been added at the first racking, no stabilising tablet would be needed as the

Campden tablet would have killed the yeast.) Similarly, when blending one wine with another a restart can occur, and there will almost certainly be a fall-out of minute particles left in the wines, however clear they may seem to be. It is advisable to leave a blended wine in the demijohn for a few days before bottling.

Remember to prepare the yeast starter at least 24 hours before preparing the must.

Remember also that a fermenting wine is best kept at an even temperature, preferably in the range of 65–75°F (18–24°C) – never above.

Do not bottle a wine until is is really clear – any sediment forming in a bottle, either caused by the presence of solids, or dead yeast cells, would be detrimental to the quality of the wine, and apart from this, would result in cloudiness when pouring.

These wines will all improve with keeping beyond the times stated in the recipes.

'Come eat of my bread and drink of the wine which I have mingled.'

Proverbs 9, verse 5

RECIPES

Apple

(a medium-sweet table wine)

Ingredients

Bordeaux or all-purpose yeast
  starter
8 lb (3.6kg) apples
Campden tablets as per
  instructions
2 lb (900g) granulated sugar
2 pints (1 litre) white grape
  juice (N.B. containing no
  preservatives)

1 3mg vitamin B_1 tablet
½ level tsp Epsom salts
  (optional)
1 level tsp nutrient salts
1 level tsp pectic enzyme

Procedure

Obtain a mixture of eating and cooking apples, including, if possible, 1 lb (450g) crab apples. Wash and crush them, either slicing and then pulping them with a block of wood, or better still, putting them through a juice extractor, in which case the quantity could be reduced to 6 lb (2.5kg). Place the crushed apples or juice immediately into a sterilised bucket with 4 pints (2 litres) of water and 1 Campden tablet. After 24 hours dissolve the sugar in 2 pints (1 litre) of hot water, add this and the remaining ingredients, making it up to 8 pints (4.5 litres) with cold water – remember this includes the yeast starter. Ferment in the bucket for 3 days, stirring daily, then strain off the fermenting must into a demijohn under airlock, topping up if necessary. Ferment to dryness in a warm place, and then rack into another jar with 1 Campden tablet. Rack again after a further 14 days. This wine is drinkable after 3–4 months, but a longer period of maturation will repay, as the wine improves considerably up to 18 months. Sweeten to taste a few days before bottling.

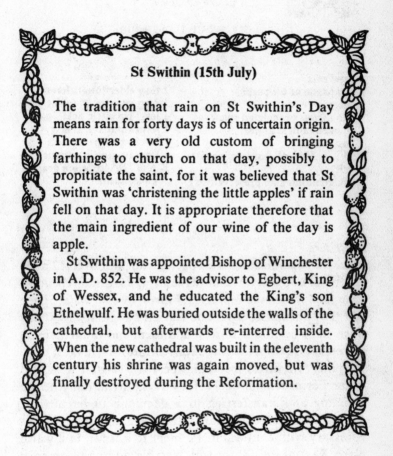

St Swithin (15th July)

The tradition that rain on St Swithin's Day means rain for forty days is of uncertain origin. There was a very old custom of bringing farthings to church on that day, possibly to propitiate the saint, for it was believed that St Swithin was 'christening the little apples' if rain fell on that day. It is appropriate therefore that the main ingredient of our wine of the day is apple.

St Swithin was appointed Bishop of Winchester in A.D. 852. He was the advisor to Egbert, King of Wessex, and he educated the King's son Ethelwulf. He was buried outside the walls of the cathedral, but afterwards re-interred inside. When the new cathedral was built in the eleventh century his shrine was again moved, but was finally destroyed during the Reformation.

Apple & Elderflower

(a dry, white table wine)

Ingredients

Champagne or all-purpose yeast
   starter
1¾ lb (800g) granulated sugar
Campden tablets as per
   instructions
1 35 fl oz (995ml) bottle of apple
   juice
(N.B. containing no preservatives)

2 tbsp elderflower florets
1 3mg vitamin B$_1$ tablet
1 level tsp citric acid
1 level tsp malic acid
1 level tsp nutrient salts
1 level tsp pectic enzyme
½ pint (285ml) white grape
   concentrate

Procedure

Place the sugar in a sterilised bucket and pour over it 2 pints
(1 litre) of hot water. Stir until the sugar has dissolved, add 1
Campden tablet and 3 pints (1.7 litres) of cold water. Then
add the apple juice, cover and leave for 24 hours. Next day
wash the elderflower florets, add them and the remaining
ingredients (except the grape concentrate) and make it up to
7½ pints (4.2 litres) including the yeast starter, with cold
water. Ferment in the bucket for 4 days, stirring daily, before
straining and transferring to a demijohn under airlock,
adding the grape concentrate at this stage, and topping up as
necessary with cold water. Ferment to a finish in a warm
place. Rack as soon as the wine is stable, adding 1 Campden
tablet. This wine is drinkable after 3–4 months, but a longer
period of maturation will repay, as the wine improves
considerably up to 18 months. Sweeten to taste a few days
before bottling.

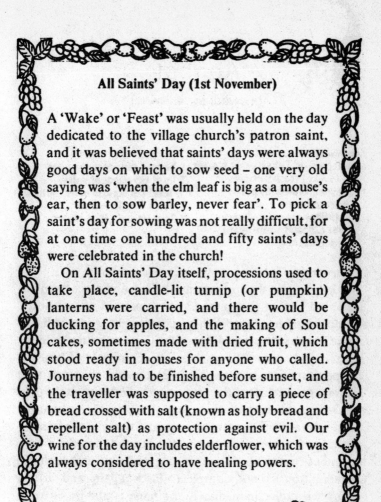

All Saints' Day (1st November)

A 'Wake' or 'Feast' was usually held on the day
dedicated to the village church's patron saint,
and it was believed that saints' days were always
good days on which to sow seed – one very old
saying was 'when the elm leaf is big as a mouse's
ear, then to sow barley, never fear'. To pick a
saint's day for sowing was not really difficult, for
at one time one hundred and fifty saints' days
were celebrated in the church!

On All Saints' Day itself, processions used to
take place, candle-lit turnip (or pumpkin)
lanterns were carried, and there would be
ducking for apples, and the making of Soul
cakes, sometimes made with dried fruit, which
stood ready in houses for anyone who called.
Journeys had to be finished before sunset, and
the traveller was supposed to carry a piece of
bread crossed with salt (known as holy bread and
repellent salt) as protection against evil. Our
wine for the day includes elderflower, which was
always considered to have healing powers.

Apricot

(a sweet social wine)

Ingredients

Sauternes or Tokay yeast starter
3 lb (1.4kg) fresh apricots
Campden tablets as per
  instructions
2 lb (900g) granulated sugar
½ pint (285ml) white grape
  concentrate

1 heaped tsp pectic enzyme
1 level tsp nutrient salts
¼ level tsp Epsom salts (optional)
½ level tsp citric acid
1 3mg vitamin B_1 tablet

Procedure

Wash and stone the apricots, mash them and place them in a sterilised bucket in 4 pints (2 litres) of cold water. Add 1 Campden tablet, cover and leave overnight. After 24 hours make it up to 7½ pints (4.2 litres) with warm water. Add the sugar, and stir until it has all dissolved. When the temperature is down to 70°F (21°C) add the remaining ingredients, including the yeast starter. Ferment on the pulp for 3 days, stirring daily, before straining the fermenting must into a demijohn under airlock. Continue the fermentation in a warm place, but watch carefully in case a pulp sediment builds up, in which case rack, even though the fermentation is not complete. Rack again and add a Campden tablet immediately the wine is stable. Store in bulk, if possible up to 12 months, racking as necessary during this time. Sweeten to taste a few days before bottling.

Note: this wine may also be made from dried fruit – if so, use 12 oz (340g) of dried apricots, washed and chopped into small pieces.

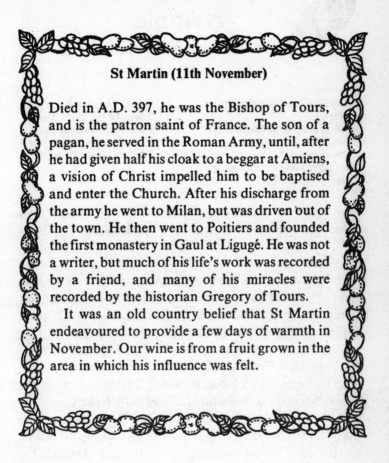

St Martin (11th November)

Died in A.D. 397, he was the Bishop of Tours, and is the patron saint of France. The son of a pagan, he served in the Roman Army, until, after he had given half his cloak to a beggar at Amiens, a vision of Christ impelled him to be baptised and enter the Church. After his discharge from the army he went to Milan, but was driven out of the town. He then went to Poitiers and founded the first monastery in Gaul at Ligugé. He was not a writer, but much of his life's work was recorded by a friend, and many of his miracles were recorded by the historian Gregory of Tours.

It was an old country belief that St Martin endeavoured to provide a few days of warmth in November. Our wine is from a fruit grown in the area in which his influence was felt.

Blackberry
& Apple
(a light-bodied medium social wine)

Ingredients

Beaujolais or all-purpose yeast starter
2½ lb (1.1kg) granulated sugar
Campden tablets as per instructions
4 lb (1.8kg) apples (including some crab apples)

3 lb (1.4kg) blackberries
1 heaped tsp citric acid
1 level tsp nutrient salts
1 level tsp pectic enzyme
1 3mg vitamin B₁ tablet

Note: taste the fruit beforehand, if it is slightly acid then reduce the amount of citric acid to one level tsp.

Procedure

Place the sugar in a sterilised bucket, and pour 2 pints (1 litre) of very hot water over it. Stir until dissolved, and add 1 Campden tablet. Then wash the fruit thoroughly, chop the apples, cutting out all the bad parts. Put the apples into the bucket, liquidise or mash the blackberries in some water and add them also. Cover and leave for 24 hours, and then make it up to 1 gallon (4.5 litres) including 2 pints (1 litre) of hot water. When the temperature is down to 70°F (21°C) add the acid, nutrient salts, pectic enzyme, vitamin B₁ tablet and the yeast starter. Stir these in and ferment on the pulp for 5 days, stirring daily, before straining off the solids and placing the liquor in a demijohn under airlock. Top up to 1½ in (38mm) from the base of the cork if necessary with cold water. Continue the fermentation to a finish in a warm place. Rack immediately on completion adding 1 Campden tablet. This wine should be ready for drinking within 4 months.

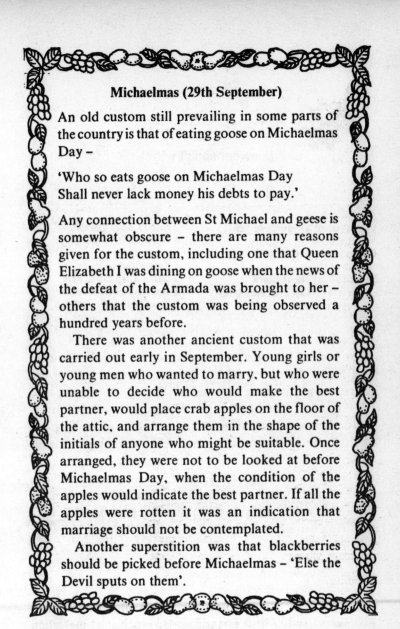

Michaelmas (29th September)

An old custom still prevailing in some parts of the country is that of eating goose on Michaelmas Day –

'Who so eats goose on Michaelmas Day
Shall never lack money his debts to pay.'

Any connection between St Michael and geese is somewhat obscure – there are many reasons given for the custom, including one that Queen Elizabeth I was dining on goose when the news of the defeat of the Armada was brought to her – others that the custom was being observed a hundred years before.

There was another ancient custom that was carried out early in September. Young girls or young men who wanted to marry, but who were unable to decide who would make the best partner, would place crab apples on the floor of the attic, and arrange them in the shape of the initials of anyone who might be suitable. Once arranged, they were not to be looked at before Michaelmas Day, when the condition of the apples would indicate the best partner. If all the apples were rotten it was an indication that marriage should not be contemplated.

Another superstition was that blackberries should be picked before Michaelmas – 'Else the Devil sputs on them'.

Black Cherry

(a sweet social wine)

Ingredients

Port-type or all-purpose yeast
  starter
Campden tablets as per
  instructions
32 oz (907g) tin of black
  cherries (N.B. containing no
  preservatives)

2½ lb (1.1kg) granulated sugar
8 fl oz (227ml) red grape
  concentrate
1 3mg vitamin B₁ tablet
1 heaped tsp citric acid
1 level tsp nutrient salts
1 level tsp pectic enzyme

Procedure

Pour 3 pints (1.7 litres) of warm water in a sterilised bucket
and add 1 Campden tablet. Extract the stones from the
cherries and place the cherries and their juice straight into
the bucket. Stir in the sugar until it has all dissolved, cover,
and leave overnight. After 24 hours make it up to 7½ pints
(4.2 litres) with warm water, and when the temperature is
down to 70°F (21°C) add the remaining ingredients,
including the yeast starter. Ferment on the pulp for 4 days,
stirring daily, before straining off the fermenting must into a
demijohn under airlock. Continue the fermentation to a
finish in a warm place, racking and adding 1 Campden tablet
as soon as the wine is stable. The wine should be ready for
drinking between 3–4 months, though it will improve with
keeping.

Note: taste the fruit beforehand, if it is slightly acid then
necessary to add a little tartaric acid (a pinch at a time) when
sweetening to taste before bottling.

New Year's Eve (31st December)

A time of celebration when the New Year is welcomed in at parties, dances, etc. – gone are the disappointments and troubles of the past, and the future is looked forward to as the time for beginning a new life with new hope.

In the Northumbrian village of Allendale the New Year is welcomed in by the preparation of a large bonfire which must not be lit until the proceedings have reached a climax. Followed by the local Silver Band, Guisers (men disguised, some as women), go round the public houses fortifying themselves. As midnight approaches a procession is formed, each man carrying a tar barrel above his head filled with paraffin-soaked shavings – these are set alight, and the Guisers encircle the bonfire and throw their barrels on it. As soon as the bonfire dies down, First Footing begins (see page 99).

This wine consisting of tinned ingredients can be made at a time of the year when fresh fruit is not available.

Blackcurrant

(a sweet social wine)

Ingredients
Bordeaux or all-purpose yeast starter
2 lb (900g) blackcurrants
3 lb (1.4kg) granulated sugar
Campden tablets as per instructions
8 fl oz (227ml) red grape concentrate
1 3mg vitamin B$_1$ tablet
1 level tsp pectic enzyme
1 level tsp nutrient salts

Procedure
Wash the blackcurrants. Liquidise or mash them in a little water and place them in a sterilised bucket, together with the sugar and 3 pints (1.7 litres) of hot water. Stir until the sugar has all dissolved, add 1 Campden tablet, cover and leave overnight. After 24 hours, make it up to 8 pints (4.5 litres) with warm water, and when the temperature is down to 70°F (21°C), add the remaining ingredients, including the yeast starter. Ferment on the pulp for 4 days, stirring daily, before straining the fermenting must into a demijohn under airlock. Rack as soon as the wine is stable, adding 1 Campden tablet, and rack a second time after 4 weeks. Sweeten to taste a few days before bottling. This wine could be drunk after 4 months.

Note: this wine may be a little harsh when young, if so add 2 tsp of glycerin to the gallon (4.5 litres) and thoroughly mix before bottling.

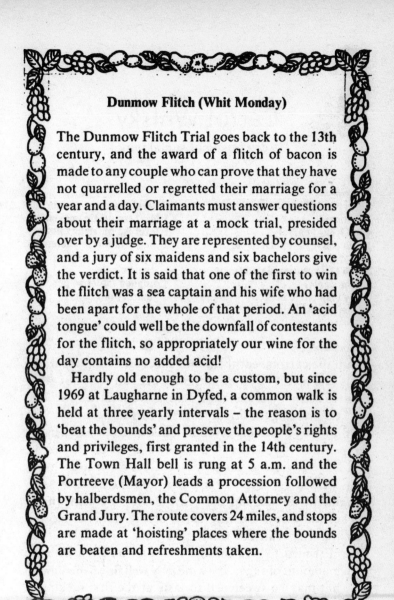

Dunmow Flitch (Whit Monday)

The Dunmow Flitch Trial goes back to the 13th century, and the award of a flitch of bacon is made to any couple who can prove that they have not quarrelled or regretted their marriage for a year and a day. Claimants must answer questions about their marriage at a mock trial, presided over by a judge. They are represented by counsel, and a jury of six maidens and six bachelors give the verdict. It is said that one of the first to win the flitch was a sea captain and his wife who had been apart for the whole of that period. An 'acid tongue' could well be the downfall of contestants for the flitch, so appropriately our wine for the day contains no added acid!

Hardly old enough to be a custom, but since 1969 at Laugharne in Dyfed, a common walk is held at three yearly intervals – the reason is to 'beat the bounds' and preserve the people's rights and privileges, first granted in the 14th century. The Town Hall bell is rung at 5 a.m. and the Portreeve (Mayor) leads a procession followed by halberdsmen, the Common Attorney and the Grand Jury. The route covers 24 miles, and stops are made at 'hoisting' places where the bounds are beaten and refreshments taken.

Carrot Whisky

(a dry or sweet social wine)

Ingredients

Sherry or all-purpose yeast
  starter
4 lb (1.8kg) carrots
1¾ lb (800g) granulated sugar
  (for dry) or
2½ lb (1.1kg) granulated sugar
  (for sweet)
1 level tsp citric acid
1 level tsp tartaric acid

½ level tsp grape tannin
1 level tsp pectic enzyme
1 level tsp nutrient salts
2 3mg vitamin B₁ tablets
½ pint (285ml) white grape
  concentrate
Campden tablet as per
  instructions

Procedure

Scrub the carrots, cut them into slices and cook them in 5 pints (2.8 litres) of water until they are soft – do not allow them to mash. Place the sugar, acids and tannin in a sterilised bucket, straining the liquor from the carrots over them. Stir until the sugar has dissolved and allow to cool. When the temperature is down to 70°F (21°C) add the pectic enzyme and leave covered overnight. Next day, make it up to 7½ pints (4.2 litres) with warm water, add the nutrient salts, vitamin B₁ tablets and the yeast starter. Ferment in the bucket for 4 days, stirring daily, before transferring to a demijohn under airlock, adding the grape concentrate at this time. Ferment to a finish in a warm place. Even with the higher amount of sugar, the wine may well finish medium to dry, but may be sweetened to taste at the first racking at which time 1 Campden tablet should be added. This wine may be drunk young but it will benefit greatly from a maturation time of up to a year.

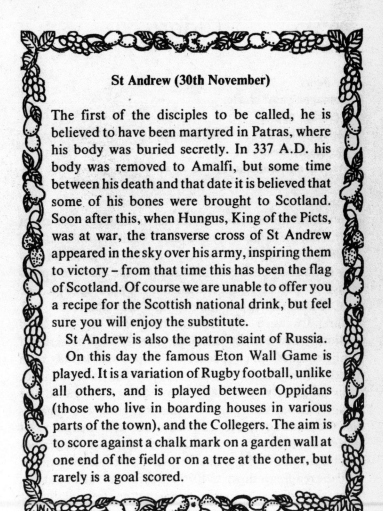

St Andrew (30th November)

The first of the disciples to be called, he is believed to have been martyred in Patras, where his body was buried secretly. In 337 A.D. his body was removed to Amalfi, but some time between his death and that date it is believed that some of his bones were brought to Scotland. Soon after this, when Hungus, King of the Picts, was at war, the transverse cross of St Andrew appeared in the sky over his army, inspiring them to victory – from that time this has been the flag of Scotland. Of course we are unable to offer you a recipe for the Scottish national drink, but feel sure you will enjoy the substitute.

St Andrew is also the patron saint of Russia.

On this day the famous Eton Wall Game is played. It is a variation of Rugby football, unlike all others, and is played between Oppidans (those who live in boarding houses in various parts of the town), and the Collegers. The aim is to score against a chalk mark on a garden wall at one end of the field or on a tree at the other, but rarely is a goal scored.

Cider

Ingredients
Champagne yeast starter
6 lb (2.5kg) apples
Campden tablets as per instructions
Sugar (as necessary)
1 level tsp nutrient salts

Procedure
Two things are of vital importance to us in the making of
cider, first, the availability of a juice extractor, otherwise the
crushing of the apples in order to extract the juice can be a
long and messy business, and secondly the blend of apples
we use, the best being one third of a sharp cooking apple, one
third of a dessert apple, and one third crab apple.

Carefully wash the fruit, cutting out any damaged
portions, then extract the juice directly into a sterilised
demijohn, into which a soluble Campden tablet has been
placed. When a gallon (4.5 litres) of juice has been obtained,
make the gravity up to 1060 s.g. by adding the sugar in 4 oz
(114g) batches (see page 47) and stir until the sugar is
dissolved, and cover. After 24 hours, add a champagne yeast
starter and the nutrient salts, and ferment until the gravity
has dropped to 1045 s.g. then rack and continue the ferment
until the reading is down to 1030 s.g. A further racking at this
stage should result in the fermentation terminating at
around 1020 s.g. – then add 2 Campden tablets and give the
cider a final racking. The cider may be drunk after 3–4
months.

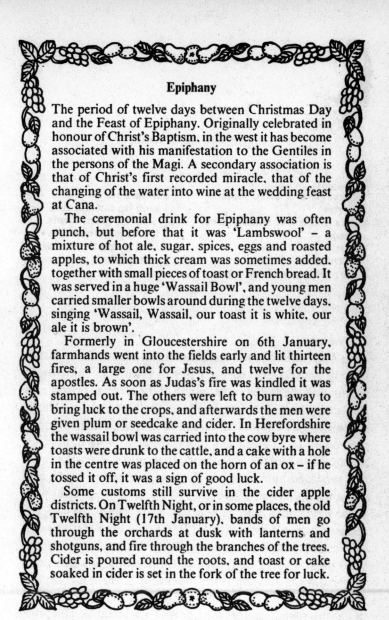

Epiphany

The period of twelve days between Christmas Day
and the Feast of Epiphany. Originally celebrated in
honour of Christ's Baptism, in the west it has become
associated with his manifestation to the Gentiles in
the persons of the Magi. A secondary association is
that of Christ's first recorded miracle, that of the
changing of the water into wine at the wedding feast
at Cana.

The ceremonial drink for Epiphany was often
punch, but before that it was 'Lambswool' – a
mixture of hot ale, sugar, spices, eggs and roasted
apples, to which thick cream was sometimes added,
together with small pieces of toast or French bread. It
was served in a huge 'Wassail Bowl', and young men
carried smaller bowls around during the twelve days,
singing 'Wassail, Wassail, our toast it is white, our
ale it is brown'.

Formerly in Gloucestershire on 6th January,
farmhands went into the fields early and lit thirteen
fires, a large one for Jesus, and twelve for the
apostles. As soon as Judas's fire was kindled it was
stamped out. The others were left to burn away to
bring luck to the crops, and afterwards the men were
given plum or seedcake and cider. In Herefordshire
the wassail bowl was carried into the cow byre where
toasts were drunk to the cattle, and a cake with a hole
in the centre was placed on the horn of an ox – if he
tossed it off, it was a sign of good luck.

Some customs still survive in the cider apple
districts. On Twelfth Night, or in some places, the old
Twelfth Night (17th January), bands of men go
through the orchards at dusk with lanterns and
shotguns, and fire through the branches of the trees.
Cider is poured round the roots, and toast or cake
soaked in cider is set in the fork of the tree for luck.

Dandelion

(a light, dry table wine)

Ingredients

Champagne or Chablis yeast
  starter
4 pints (2 litres) dandelion flower
  heads
Campden tablet as per
  instructions
1¾ lb (800g) granulated sugar

1 heaped tsp citric acid
1 level tsp tartaric acid
½ level tsp grape tannin
1 level tsp nutrient salts
1 level tsp pectic enzyme
½ pint (285ml) white grape
  concentrate

Procedure

Take 4 one-pint (½ litre) containers of dandelion flower heads
loosely packed, picked on a dry day when in full flower.
Remove all the stalks and as much of the green as possible, as
this can cause bitterness. Place the flowers in a large
container in 4 pints (2 litres) of boiling water. Add 1
Campden tablet and leave them to steep for 48 hours (not
more). Then boil the mixture for 10 minutes. Place the sugar
in a sterilised bucket, strain the liquor on to the sugar, and
stir until dissolved. Make it up to 7½ pints (4.2 litres) with
cold water and add the acids and tannin. When the
temperature is down to 70°F (21°C), add the nutrient salts,
pectic enzyme and yeast starter. Stir well, cover, and ferment
for 3 days, stirring daily, before transferring to a demijohn
under airlock. As soon as the first heavy ferment is complete
(about 5 days) stir in the concentrate, and ferment to a finish
in a warm place. Rack as soon as the wine is stable. This wine
can be drunk after 3–4 months.

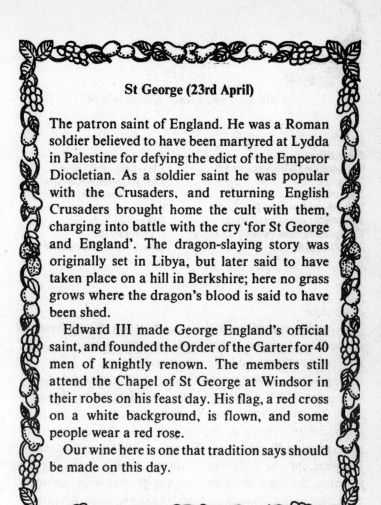

St George (23rd April)

The patron saint of England. He was a Roman soldier believed to have been martyred at Lydda in Palestine for defying the edict of the Emperor Diocletian. As a soldier saint he was popular with the Crusaders, and returning English Crusaders brought home the cult with them, charging into battle with the cry 'for St George and England'. The dragon-slaying story was originally set in Libya, but later said to have taken place on a hill in Berkshire; here no grass grows where the dragon's blood is said to have been shed.

Edward III made George England's official saint, and founded the Order of the Garter for 40 men of knightly renown. The members still attend the Chapel of St George at Windsor in their robes on his feast day. His flag, a red cross on a white background, is flown, and some people wear a red rose.

Our wine here is one that tradition says should be made on this day.

Date

(a full-bodied, sweet social wine)

Ingredients

Madeira or all-purpose yeast
  starter
2 lb (900g) dates
1 lb (450g) bananas (mashed)
1 lb (450g) granulated sugar
Campden tablets as per
  instructions

2 level tsp citric acid
1 level tsp nutrient salts
1 3mg vitamin B_1 tablet
1 level tsp pectic enzyme
8 fl oz (227ml) white grape
  concentrate
Invert sugar as required

Procedure

Thoroughly wash the dates in a little water. Chop them up
and place them in a sterilised bucket together with the
mashed bananas. Add the sugar and 3 pints (1.7 litres) of
boiling water, and stir until the sugar has dissolved. Add 1
Campden tablet, cover and leave overnight. After 24 hours
make it up to 7 pints (4 litres) with warm water, and when the
temperature is down to 70°F (21°C), add the acid, nutrient
salts, vitamin B_1 tablet, pectic enzyme and the yeast starter.
Ferment on the pulp for 5 days, stirring daily, before
straining the must into a demijohn under airlock, topping up
with the grape concentrate and cold water as necessary.
Continue the fermentation in a warm place, and as long as
the yeast is working add invert sugar in ¼ pint (142ml) lots
each time the gravity drops to 1006. Rack immediately on
completion of the ferment, adding 1 Campden tablet. This
wine may be drunk after 4 months.

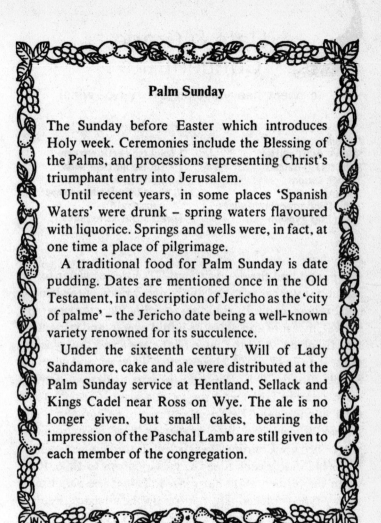

Palm Sunday

The Sunday before Easter which introduces Holy week. Ceremonies include the Blessing of the Palms, and processions representing Christ's triumphant entry into Jerusalem.

Until recent years, in some places 'Spanish Waters' were drunk – spring waters flavoured with liquorice. Springs and wells were, in fact, at one time a place of pilgrimage.

A traditional food for Palm Sunday is date pudding. Dates are mentioned once in the Old Testament, in a description of Jericho as the 'city of palme' – the Jericho date being a well-known variety renowned for its succulence.

Under the sixteenth century Will of Lady Sandamore, cake and ale were distributed at the Palm Sunday service at Hentland, Sellack and Kings Cadel near Ross on Wye. The ale is no longer given, but small cakes, bearing the impression of the Paschal Lamb are still given to each member of the congregation.

Date & Grape Concentrate

(a sweet, heavy-bodied, sherry-type wine)

Ingredients

Sherry yeast starter
3 lb (1.4kg) dates
2 large lemons
2 oranges
1 lb (450g) granulated sugar
1 oz (28g) gypsum

1 level tsp pectic enzyme
1 level tsp nutrient salts
1 3mg vitamin B$_1$ tablet
½ pint (285ml) white grape
 concentrate
Invert sugar as required

Procedure

Chop, and boil the dates in 3 pts/1.7 litres of water for 30 minutes, together with the thinly pared rinds of the lemons and oranges, carefully avoiding any pith. Place the sugar in a bucket, measure and pour the liquid over it, and stir until it has dissolved. Add the juice of the fruit and the gypsum, make it up to 7½ pts/4.2 litres with cold water, and when the temperature is 70°F/21°C add the pectic enzyme, nutrient salts, vitamin tablet and the yeast starter. Ferment for 4 days, stirring daily, before straining into a demijohn under airlock, adding the grape concentrate. Note: the demijohn is *not* topped up. Continue the ferment, but add invert sugar in ¼ pt/142ml lots each time the gravity drops to 1006. Rack when the fermentation has ceased. This is the *only* time a sherry-type is racked. Do not top up the airspace. Replace the airlock with a wad of cotton wool. Taste from time to time to ensure the oxidation is not overdone. When ready, replace the cotton wool with an airlock and store in bulk until required. This wine may be drunk after 6 months.

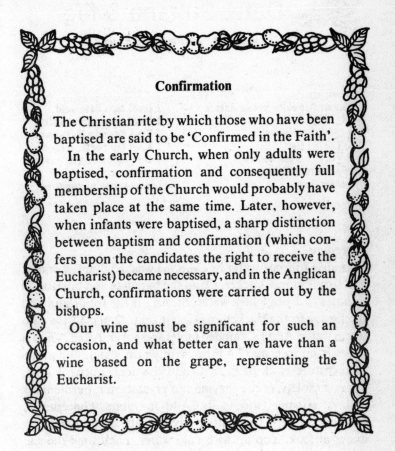

Confirmation

The Christian rite by which those who have been baptised are said to be 'Confirmed in the Faith'.

In the early Church, when only adults were baptised, confirmation and consequently full membership of the Church would probably have taken place at the same time. Later, however, when infants were baptised, a sharp distinction between baptism and confirmation (which confers upon the candidates the right to receive the Eucharist) became necessary, and in the Anglican Church, confirmations were carried out by the bishops.

Our wine must be significant for such an occasion, and what better can we have than a wine based on the grape, representing the Eucharist.

Date, Sultana & Fig

(a sweet, white dessert wine)

Ingredients

Tokay or Madeira yeast starter
½ lb (227g) dates
2 lb (900g) sultanas
½ lb (227g) figs
¼ lb (114g) dried bananas
Campden tablets as per
    instructions

1 level tsp citric acid
1 level tsp nutrient salts
2 3mg vitamin B$_1$ tablets
1 level tsp pectic enzyme
1 tin (700ml) white grape
    concentrate
Invert sugar as required

Procedure

Liquidise in some water or chop the washed dates, sultanas and figs. Put in a bucket. Chop the bananas and boil for 25 minutes in 1 pt/½ litre water. Strain off the solids and add the liquor to the bucket, making it up to 2 pts/1 litre with warm water. Add 1 Campden tablet and cover. After 24 hours make it up to 6 pts/3.4 litres with warm water. When the temperature is at 70°F/21°C add the acid, nutrient salts, vitamin tablets, pectic enzyme and yeast starter. Ferment for 3 days, stirring twice daily. Add the grape concentrate. Ferment and stir for 2 more days. Strain into a demijohn under airlock. Top up with cold water. Each time the s.g. drops to 1010 add ¼ pt/142ml invert sugar. At the end of the ferment adjust the final s.g. to 1040 and add any extra tartaric acid (a pinch at a time) that may be needed. Rack when stable adding 1 Campden tablet. Rack again after a month. This wine may be drunk after 6 months.

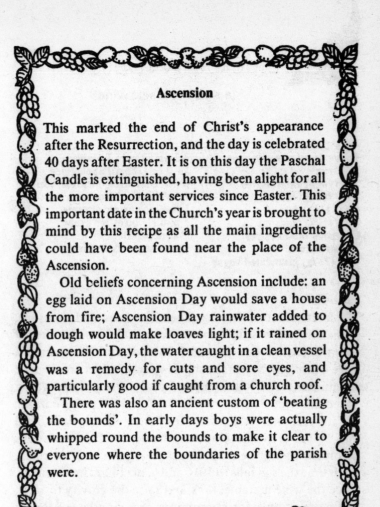

Ascension

This marked the end of Christ's appearance after the Resurrection, and the day is celebrated 40 days after Easter. It is on this day the Paschal Candle is extinguished, having been alight for all the more important services since Easter. This important date in the Church's year is brought to mind by this recipe as all the main ingredients could have been found near the place of the Ascension.

Old beliefs concerning Ascension include: an egg laid on Ascension Day would save a house from fire; Ascension Day rainwater added to dough would make loaves light; if it rained on Ascension Day, the water caught in a clean vessel was a remedy for cuts and sore eyes, and particularly good if caught from a church roof.

There was also an ancient custom of 'beating the bounds'. In early days boys were actually whipped round the bounds to make it clear to everyone where the boundaries of the parish were.

Elderberry (Dessert)

(a sweet dessert wine)

Ingredients

Tokay or all-purpose yeast
   starter
2 lb (900g) elderberries
2 lb (900g) blackberries
4 oz (114g) dates
1 lb (450g) damsons
Campden tablet as per
   instructions
½ lb (227g) granulated sugar

1 3mg vitamin B₁ tablet
10 fl oz (285ml) apple juice
(N.B. containing no preservatives)
1 level tsp nutrient salts
1 level tsp pectic enzyme
1 pint (½ litre) red grape
   concentrate
Invert sugar as required

Procedure

Wash the elderberries, blackberries, dates and damsons.
Stone the damsons. Place all the fruit with 5 pts/2.8 litres of
warm water in a bucket, add 1 Campden tablet, cover and
leave overnight. Stir in the sugar, vitamin tablet, apple juice
and nutrient salts. Make it up to 7 pts/4 litres with hot water.
When the temperature is 70°F/21°C add the pectic enzyme
and the yeast starter. Ferment for 3 days, stirring daily. Add
the grape concentrate. Continue the ferment for 2 more days
before straining the must into a demijohn under airlock.
Each time the s.g. falls to 1010 add ¼ pt/142ml invert sugar.
Once the wine is stable, rack and raise the gravity to 1030,
and store in bulk for a minimum of 6 months – a longer
maturation period is even better.

Note: largely dependent on the ripeness of the fruit used, it
may be necessary to add a little acid to the wine in order to
balance the final sweetness.

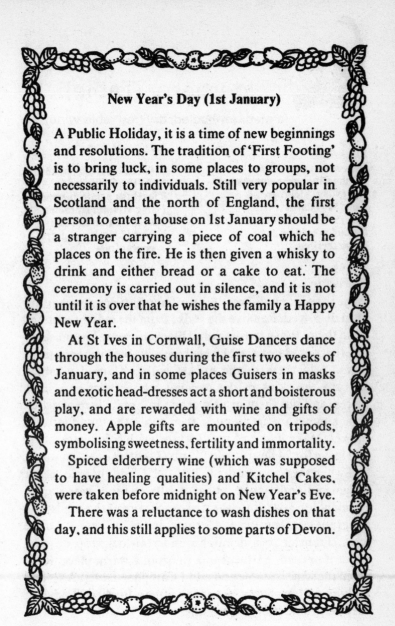

New Year's Day (1st January)

A Public Holiday, it is a time of new beginnings and resolutions. The tradition of 'First Footing' is to bring luck, in some places to groups, not necessarily to individuals. Still very popular in Scotland and the north of England, the first person to enter a house on 1st January should be a stranger carrying a piece of coal which he places on the fire. He is then given a whisky to drink and either bread or a cake to eat. The ceremony is carried out in silence, and it is not until it is over that he wishes the family a Happy New Year.

At St Ives in Cornwall, Guise Dancers dance through the houses during the first two weeks of January, and in some places Guisers in masks and exotic head-dresses act a short and boisterous play, and are rewarded with wine and gifts of money. Apple gifts are mounted on tripods, symbolising sweetness, fertility and immortality.

Spiced elderberry wine (which was supposed to have healing qualities) and Kitchel Cakes, were taken before midnight on New Year's Eve.

There was a reluctance to wash dishes on that day, and this still applies to some parts of Devon.

Elderberry (Table)

(a medium-bodied, dry, red table wine)

Ingredients

Burgundy yeast starter
1½ lb (680g) granulated sugar
2 lb (900g) elderberries
2 oz (56g) dates
2 oz (56g) blackcurrants
Campden tablets as per
  instructions

½ lb (227g) fresh bananas
1 level tsp citric acid
1 level tsp pectic enzyme
1 3mg vitamin B_1 tablet
1 level tsp nutrient salts
½ pint (285ml) red grape
  concentrate

Procedure

Place the sugar and 2 pts/1 litre of hot water in a bucket; stir until dissolved. Remove the stalks from the elderberries and wash them. Wash the dates and blackcurrants. Liquidise the elderberries, dates and blackcurrants in some water or mash them. Add them to the bucket with 1 Campden tablet. Discard the skins of the bananas, chop them into small pieces, and put them in a saucepan in 1 pt/½ litre of water. Boil, simmer for 20 minutes, then strain the liquid into the bucket. Make it up to 5 pts/2.8 litres with cold water, cover and leave for 24 hours. Add 2½ pts/1.4 litres of warm water, and when the temperature is 70°F/21°C add the acid, pectic enzyme, vitamin tablet, nutrient salts and the yeast starter. Ferment for 3 days in a warm place. Strain off the solids, add the grape concentrate, and ferment in the bucket for 2 more days. Transfer to a demijohn under airlock; top up with water if needed. Ferment to a finish in a warm place. Rack when the wine is stable and add 1 Campden tablet. A second racking will probably be needed after a further 28 days. It may be drunk after 4–6 months.

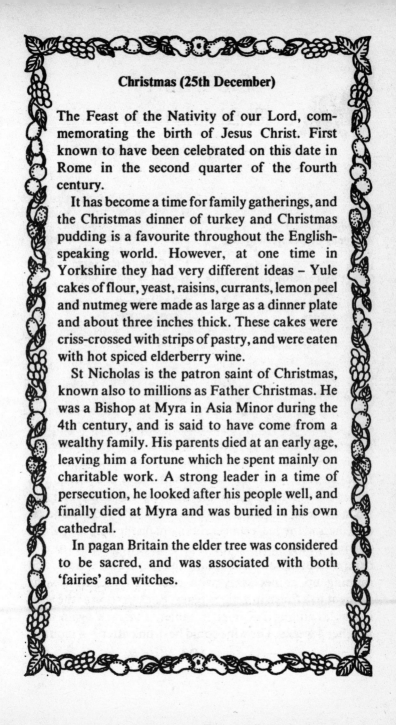

Christmas (25th December)

The Feast of the Nativity of our Lord, commemorating the birth of Jesus Christ. First known to have been celebrated on this date in Rome in the second quarter of the fourth century.

It has become a time for family gatherings, and the Christmas dinner of turkey and Christmas pudding is a favourite throughout the English-speaking world. However, at one time in Yorkshire they had very different ideas – Yule cakes of flour, yeast, raisins, currants, lemon peel and nutmeg were made as large as a dinner plate and about three inches thick. These cakes were criss-crossed with strips of pastry, and were eaten with hot spiced elderberry wine.

St Nicholas is the patron saint of Christmas, known also to millions as Father Christmas. He was a Bishop at Myra in Asia Minor during the 4th century, and is said to have come from a wealthy family. His parents died at an early age, leaving him a fortune which he spent mainly on charitable work. A strong leader in a time of persecution, he looked after his people well, and finally died at Myra and was buried in his own cathedral.

In pagan Britain the elder tree was considered to be sacred, and was associated with both 'fairies' and witches.

Elderberry & Blackberry

(a light, dry, Italian-type table wine)

Ingredients

Burgundy or Beaujolais yeast
starter
1¼ lb (570g) blackberries
6 oz (170g) elderberries
1 large peeled banana
Campden tablets as per
instructions

1¾ lb (800g) granulated sugar
1 level tsp nutrient salts
1 level tsp tartaric acid
1 3mg vitamin B₁ tablet
1 level tsp pectic enzyme
8 fl oz (227ml) red grape
concentrate

Procedure

Wash the fruit. Liquidise it or mash it in 2 pints (1 litre) of
cold water. Place it in a sterilised bucket, add 1 Campden
tablet, cover, and leave it for 24 hours. Then dissolve the
sugar in 3 pints (1.7 litres) of hot water, and add it to the
fruit, together with the nutrient salts, acid and vitamin B_1
tablet. Make it up to 7½ pints (4.2 litres) with cold water and
when the temperature is down to 70°F (21°C) add the pectic
enzyme and the yeast starter. Ferment on the pulp for 3 days,
stirring daily, then strain the fermenting must into a
demijohn under airlock, adding the grape concentrate, and
topping up as necessary with cold water. Continue the
ferment to a finish in a warm place. Rack as soon as the wine
is stable, adding 1 Campden tablet, and rack again after
another 4 weeks. The wine could be drunk after 3–4 months.

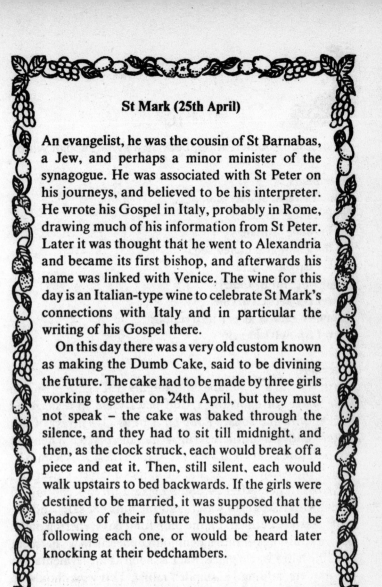

St Mark (25th April)

An evangelist, he was the cousin of St Barnabas, a Jew, and perhaps a minor minister of the synagogue. He was associated with St Peter on his journeys, and believed to be his interpreter. He wrote his Gospel in Italy, probably in Rome, drawing much of his information from St Peter. Later it was thought that he went to Alexandria and became its first bishop, and afterwards his name was linked with Venice. The wine for this day is an Italian-type wine to celebrate St Mark's connections with Italy and in particular the writing of his Gospel there.

On this day there was a very old custom known as making the Dumb Cake, said to be divining the future. The cake had to be made by three girls working together on 24th April, but they must not speak – the cake was baked through the silence, and they had to sit till midnight, and then, as the clock struck, each would break off a piece and eat it. Then, still silent, each would walk upstairs to bed backwards. If the girls were destined to be married, it was supposed that the shadow of their future husbands would be following each one, or would be heard later knocking at their bedchambers.

Fig

(a medium-bodied wine, best as a sweet social wine)

Ingredients
Madeira yeast starter
1½ lb (680g) dried figs
1½ lb (680g) sultanas
1½ lb (680g) granulated sugar
2 level tsp citric acid
1 3mg vitamin B₁ tablet
1 level tsp pectic enzyme
Campden tablets as per instructions
1 level tsp nutrient salts

Procedure
Wash the figs and sultanas thoroughly. Liquidise them in a
little water (or chop them) and place them in a sterilised
bucket with the sugar. Pour on 3 pints (1.7 litres) of hot
water, and stir until the sugar has dissolved. When the
temperature is down to 70°F (21°C) add the acid, vitamin B₁
tablet, the pectic enzyme and 1 Campden tablet. Cover and
leave overnight. After 24 hours make it up to 1 gallon (4.5
litres) with lukewarm water, add the nutrient salts and the
yeast starter. Ferment on the pulp for 4 days, stirring daily,
before straining off into a demijohn under airlock. Ferment
to a finish in a warm place. Rack as soon as the fermentation
is complete, adding 1 Campden tablet. This wine should be
sweetened to taste when ready for bottling and could be
drunk after 4 months.

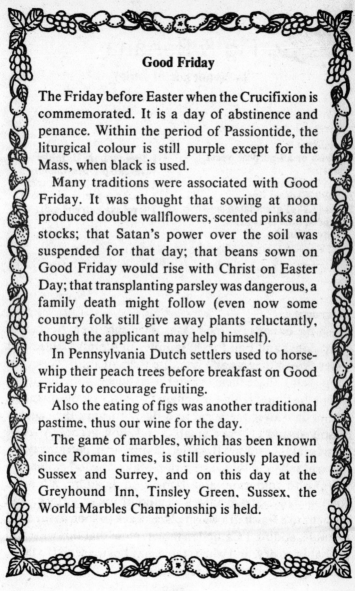

Good Friday

The Friday before Easter when the Crucifixion is commemorated. It is a day of abstinence and penance. Within the period of Passiontide, the liturgical colour is still purple except for the Mass, when black is used.

Many traditions were associated with Good Friday. It was thought that sowing at noon produced double wallflowers, scented pinks and stocks; that Satan's power over the soil was suspended for that day; that beans sown on Good Friday would rise with Christ on Easter Day; that transplanting parsley was dangerous, a family death might follow (even now some country folk still give away plants reluctantly, though the applicant may help himself).

In Pennsylvania Dutch settlers used to horse-whip their peach trees before breakfast on Good Friday to encourage fruiting.

Also the eating of figs was another traditional pastime, thus our wine for the day.

The game of marbles, which has been known since Roman times, is still seriously played in Sussex and Surrey, and on this day at the Greyhound Inn, Tinsley Green, Sussex, the World Marbles Championship is held.

Fig & Banana

(a sweet social wine)

Ingredients

Madeira or all-purpose yeast
  starter
2 lb (900g) bananas
2 lb (900g) dried figs
2½ lb (1.1kg) granulated sugar
Campden tablets as per
  instructions

1 3mg vitamin B_1 tablet
½ level tsp grape tannin
1 heaped tsp tartaric acid
1 level tsp pectic enzyme
1 level tsp nutrient salts

Procedure

Wash the bananas in their skins, then slice them (including
their skins) and boil for 30 minutes in 4 pints (2 litres) of
water. Wash the figs and liquidise them in a little water (or
chop them). Place them in a sterilised bucket with the sugar.
Strain the liquor from the bananas, measuring the quantity,
and pour it over the sugar and figs. Stir until the sugar is
dissolved, add 1 Campden tablet and allow to cool. After 24
hours add the vitamin B_1 tablet, tannin, acid, pectic enzyme,
nutrient salts and the yeast starter. Make it up to 1 gallon (4.5
litres) with cold water and ferment on the pulp for 5 days,
stirring daily. Strain into a demijohn under airlock, and
ferment to a finish in a warm place. Rack as soon as the wine
is stable, adding 1 Campden tablet. Note that this wine will
probably go dry, and when stable may be sweetened to taste.
It could be drunk after 4 months.

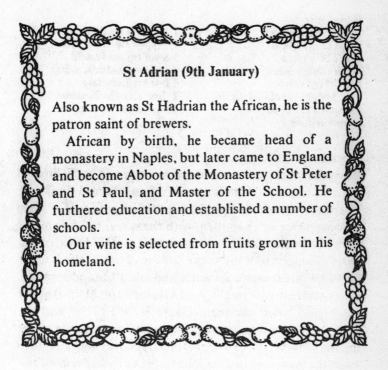

St Adrian (9th January)

Also known as St Hadrian the African, he is the patron saint of brewers.

African by birth, he became head of a monastery in Naples, but later came to England and become Abbot of the Monastery of St Peter and St Paul, and Master of the School. He furthered education and established a number of schools.

Our wine is selected from fruits grown in his homeland.

Fig, Date & Raisin

(a sweet, full-bodied social wine)

Ingredients

Tokay yeast starter
½ lb (227g) wheat
½ lb (227g) figs
1½ lb (680g) dates
1 lb (450g) raisins
2 lb (900g) granulated sugar
Campden tablet as per
  instructions

1 level tsp pectic enzyme
1 heaped tsp citric acid
1 level tsp malic acid
1 level tsp nutrient salts
1 level tsp amylase
1 3mg vitamin B₁ tablet
Invert sugar as required

Procedure

Wash the wheat and soak it overnight in one pt (½ litre) of water to soften it. Next day strain off and discard the liquid. Thoroughly wash the figs, dates and raisins. Liquidise them in some water or chop them with the wheat before placing them in a bucket. Add the sugar and 3 pts (1.7 litres) of hot water, and stir until the sugar has dissolved. Make it up to 6 pts (3.4 litres) with cold water and add 1 Campden tablet. Cover and leave overnight. Add a further 2 pts (1 litre) of hot water, and when the temperature is 70°F/21°C add the pectic enzyme, acids, nutrient salts, amylase, vitamin tablet and the yeast starter. Ferment for 5 days, stirring daily, then strain the liquor into a demijohn under airlock. Ferment to a finish in a warm place. Rack as soon as the wine is stable. This is a strong, full-bodied wine, and if it is fed with further quantities of invert sugar at the rate of ¼ pt (142ml) each time the s.g. drops to 1006, it may well become a golden dessert wine. It may be drunk after 6–9 months.

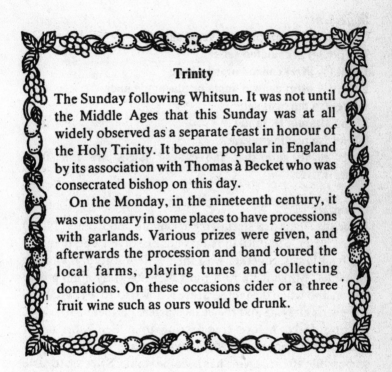

Trinity

The Sunday following Whitsun. It was not until the Middle Ages that this Sunday was at all widely observed as a separate feast in honour of the Holy Trinity. It became popular in England by its association with Thomas à Becket who was consecrated bishop on this day.

On the Monday, in the nineteenth century, it was customary in some places to have processions with garlands. Various prizes were given, and afterwards the procession and band toured the local farms, playing tunes and collecting donations. On these occasions cider or a three fruit wine such as ours would be drunk.

Fruit Juice

(a light, medium-sweet table wine)

Ingredients
Champagne or all-purpose yeast starter
2 lb (900g) granulated sugar
1 pint ($\frac{1}{2}$ litre) canned orange juice
1 pint ($\frac{1}{2}$ litre) canned apple or pineapple juice
1 level tsp nutrient salts
1 3mg vitamin B$_1$ tablet
1 level tsp pectic enzyme
Note: make sure that the canned juices are free from preservatives.

Procedure
Place the sugar in a sterilised bucket and add 2 pints (1 litre) of hot water. Stir until the sugar has dissolved, and then add the fruit juices, together with the nutrient salts and vitamin B$_1$ tablet. Make it up to 8 pints (4.5 litres) by adding cold water, and when the temperature is down to 70°F (21°C) add the pectic enzyme and the yeast starter. Ferment for 4 days, stirring daily, before transferring to a demijohn under airlock. Ferment to a finish in a warm place, racking as soon as possible after the wine has become stable. Sweeten to taste a few days before bottling. This wine could be drunk after 3 months.

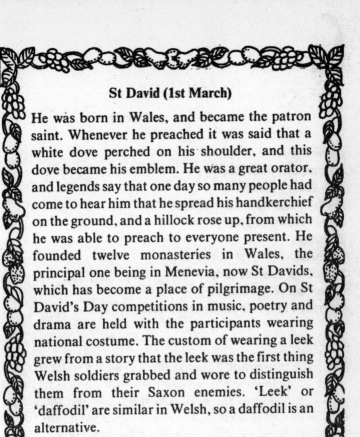

St David (1st March)

He was born in Wales, and became the patron
saint. Whenever he preached it was said that a
white dove perched on his shoulder, and this
dove became his emblem. He was a great orator,
and legends say that one day so many people had
come to hear him that he spread his handkerchief
on the ground, and a hillock rose up, from which
he was able to preach to everyone present. He
founded twelve monasteries in Wales, the
principal one being in Menevia, now St Davids,
which has become a place of pilgrimage. On St
David's Day competitions in music, poetry and
drama are held with the participants wearing
national costume. The custom of wearing a leek
grew from a story that the leek was the first thing
Welsh soldiers grabbed and wore to distinguish
them from their Saxon enemies. 'Leek' or
'daffodil' are similar in Welsh, so a daffodil is an
alternative.

A popular dish for St David's Day was
'Snowdon Pudding', a boiled suet pudding with
raisins and marmalade, and served with a little
white sauce – hence our white wine for the day.

Ginger

(a sweet social wine)

Ingredients

All-purpose yeast starter
$\frac{1}{2}$ lb (227g) raisins
$2\frac{1}{2}$ lb (1.1kg) granulated sugar
4 oz (114g) root ginger
2 oranges
2 lemons
1 level tsp nutrient salts
1 level tsp pectic enzyme
Campden tablet as per instructions

Procedure

Wash the raisins and liquidise them in a little water or chop them. Place them in a large saucepan with 6 pints (3.4 litres) of water. Bring to the boil, add the sugar and the ginger (which should be well-crushed), stir well and simmer for 30 minutes. Pour this into a sterilised bucket, measuring the quantity of liquid left after boiling. Make it up to 8 pints (4.5 litres) with cold water, and add the juice of the oranges and lemons, and the thinly peeled rinds, carefully avoiding any of the white pith. Add the nutrient salts, and when the temperature is down to 70°F (21°C) add the pectic enzyme and the yeast starter. Ferment on the pulp for 5 days, stirring daily, before straining into a demijohn under airlock. Ferment to a finish in a warm place, racking as soon as the wine is stable. Add 1 Campden tablet and sweeten to taste. This wine may be drunk after 4 months.

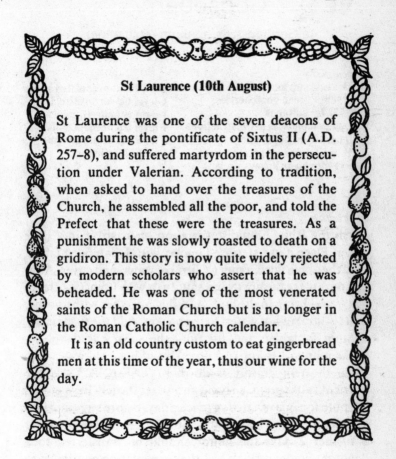

St Laurence (10th August)

St Laurence was one of the seven deacons of
Rome during the pontificate of Sixtus II (A.D.
257–8), and suffered martyrdom in the persecution under Valerian. According to tradition,
when asked to hand over the treasures of the
Church, he assembled all the poor, and told the
Prefect that these were the treasures. As a
punishment he was slowly roasted to death on a
gridiron. This story is now quite widely rejected
by modern scholars who assert that he was
beheaded. He was one of the most venerated
saints of the Roman Church but is no longer in
the Roman Catholic Church calendar.

It is an old country custom to eat gingerbread
men at this time of the year, thus our wine for the
day.

Gooseberry

(a German-type medium table wine)

Ingredients

Hock yeast starter
2 lb (900g) green gooseberries
½ lb (227g) sultanas
Campden tablets as per instructions
35 fl oz/995ml apple juice
(N.B. containing no preservatives)
4 oz (114g) clear honey

1 lb (450g) granulated sugar
1 level tsp tartaric acid
1 3mg vitamin B_1 tablet
1 level tsp nutrient salts
1 level tsp pectic enzyme
1 tbsp elderflowers

Procedure

Wash the fruit. Liquidise (or chop or mash) it in a little water. Place it in a sterilised bucket with 1 Campden tablet. Add the apple juice, a pint (½ litre) of water, and cover. After 24 hours place the honey in a saucepan with 1 pint (½ litre) of water and bring to the boil. Add this, together with another pint (½ litre) of hot water, to the bucket. Add the sugar, acid, vitamin B_1 tablet, and stir until the sugar has dissolved. Make it up to 1 gallon (4.5 litres) by adding cold water, and when the temperature is down to 70°F (21°C) add the nutrient salts, pectic enzyme and yeast starter. Ferment on the pulp for 2 days, stirring twice a day, before straining into a *second* sterilised bucket and adding the elderflowers. After a further 2 days the liquor should be transferred to a demijohn under airlock and the fermentation continued to completion in a warm place. Carry out the first racking when the gravity is down to 1006, adding 1 Campden tablet, and rack again 28 days later. This wine could be drunk after 3–4 months.

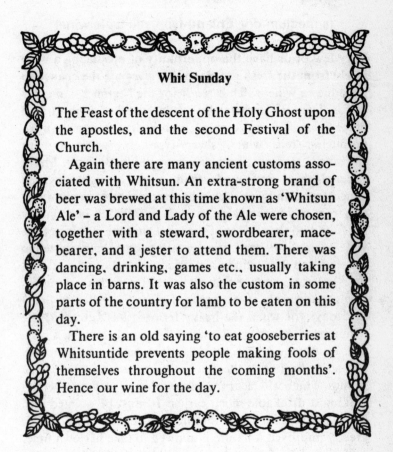

Whit Sunday

The Feast of the descent of the Holy Ghost upon the apostles, and the second Festival of the Church.

Again there are many ancient customs associated with Whitsun. An extra-strong brand of beer was brewed at this time known as 'Whitsun Ale' – a Lord and Lady of the Ale were chosen, together with a steward, swordbearer, macebearer, and a jester to attend them. There was dancing, drinking, games etc., usually taking place in barns. It was also the custom in some parts of the country for lamb to be eaten on this day.

There is an old saying 'to eat gooseberries at Whitsuntide prevents people making fools of themselves throughout the coming months'. Hence our wine for the day.

Grape

(a medium-dry, Chianti-type, red table wine)

Very few of us have the opportunity of producing a wine solely from the fresh grape, so this gives me the chance to introduce a wine which is *really* for the beginner – in other words, from a commercially-produced tin of concentrated grape juice. There are many brands on the market now, producing red, white, sherry-type etc. wines and to endeavour to draw comparisons would be difficult. I have selected this wine, made from a tin of light dry red concentrate, and you should have no problem in obtaining this from any winemaking shop. Normally full instructions are found on the reverse of the label, and the making of the wine is simplicity itself. Fermentation is generally started in the sterilised demijohn under airlock with about 5 pints (2.8 litres) of water and the contents of the tin, with a few ounces of sugar added at 2 stages during the ferment. After the first 4 or 5 days (or when the heavy ferment has subsided) the demijohn is topped up with water. Obviously racking is easy, as it is only the dead yeast cells which have to be removed, and some brands of these concentrates even include wine finings, which will clear the wine within a few days, thereby making it drinkable much earlier. It must be pointed out, however, that it does not 'mature' quicker, and it will still be greatly improved if nature is allowed to take her own time.

If a packet of yeast is not included, I would suggest a Burgundy or Beaujolais yeast for this type of wine.

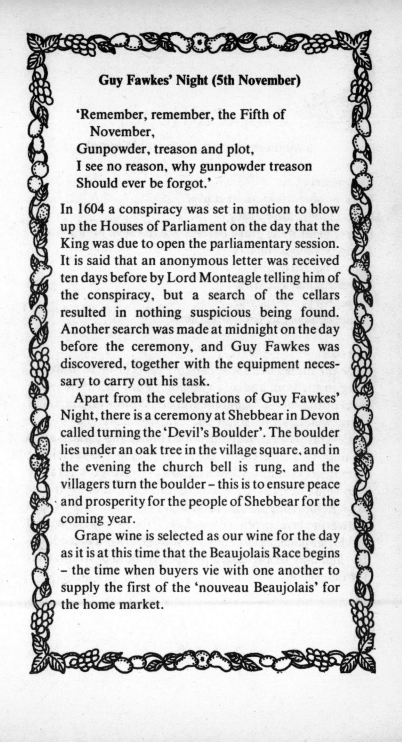

Guy Fawkes' Night (5th November)

'Remember, remember, the Fifth of
    November,
Gunpowder, treason and plot,
I see no reason, why gunpowder treason
Should ever be forgot.'

In 1604 a conspiracy was set in motion to blow
up the Houses of Parliament on the day that the
King was due to open the parliamentary session.
It is said that an anonymous letter was received
ten days before by Lord Monteagle telling him of
the conspiracy, but a search of the cellars
resulted in nothing suspicious being found.
Another search was made at midnight on the day
before the ceremony, and Guy Fawkes was
discovered, together with the equipment necessary to carry out his task.

Apart from the celebrations of Guy Fawkes'
Night, there is a ceremony at Shebbear in Devon
called turning the 'Devil's Boulder'. The boulder
lies under an oak tree in the village square, and in
the evening the church bell is rung, and the
villagers turn the boulder – this is to ensure peace
and prosperity for the people of Shebbear for the
coming year.

Grape wine is selected as our wine for the day
as it is at this time that the Beaujolais Race begins
– the time when buyers vie with one another to
supply the first of the 'nouveau Beaujolais' for
the home market.

Grape & Honey

(a medium-bodied, white table wine)

Ingredients
Hock or all-purpose yeast starter
12 oz (340g) clover honey
1 tin (700ml) white grape concentrate (medium or dry type)
2 3mg vitamin B_1 tablets
¼ level tsp citric acid
1 level tsp nutrient salts
1 level tsp pectic enzyme
Campden tablet as per instructions

Procedure
Place the honey in a saucepan in 2 pints (1 litre) of water, bring to the boil, and allow to cool. Pour the white grape concentrate into a demijohn and add 3 pints (1.7 litres) of warm water, swilling out the can to ensure that all the concentrate is used. Add the boiled honey and make it up to 1 gallon (4.5 litres) with cold water. Add the remaining ingredients including the yeast starter when the temperature is down to 70°F (21°C). Ferment for 5 days, shaking the jar daily, before topping up with cold water. Ferment to a finish in a warm place, racking immediately the wine is stable, and add 1 Campden tablet. The wine should ferment to medium-dry, and may be sweetened to taste. It could be drunk after 3–4 months.

St Ambrose (4th April)

Born 340 A.D. in Germany, he went to Rome to study Law, and ultimately became Bishop of Milan where he needed all his tact and 'honey-sweet eloquence' to deal with the many heresies prevalent at that time. There is a story that when a child, the bees crawled in and out of his mouth without stinging him. This was taken as a sign that his words would always be as sweet as honey. He is one of the patron saints of beekeepers, together with St Bernard of Clairvaux, and they were known as the honey-sweet doctors.

Until the 18th century honey was the principal sweetener, and figured in preserving of all kinds. One very old variation of a mead recipe is as follows: 'Quinces placed in a wide-necked flagon covered with willow twigs and filled up with the best and most fluid honey'. The liquid resulting from this is called Melomel or Melomeli, and is very good for invalids – our recipe for the day has many advantages, and you don't even have to be an invalid to appreciate it!

Grapefruit

(a dry aperitif wine)

Ingredients
Tokay yeast starter
9 small grapefruits
Campden tablets as per instructions
12 oz (340g) sultanas
1 level tsp pectic enzyme
1 level tsp nutrient salts
1 3mg vitamin B$_1$ tablet
2$\frac{1}{2}$ lb (1.1kg) sugar

Procedure
Cut the grapefruits in half, extract the juice, and place it in a sterilised bucket with 1 soluble Campden tablet. After 24 hours wash the dried fruit thoroughly. Liquidise it in a little water or chop it, and add it to the juice, together with the pectic enzyme, nutrient salts, vitamin B$_1$ tablet and 1$\frac{1}{2}$ lb (680g) of the sugar. Make it up to 6 pints (3.4 litres) with tepid water, add the yeast starter, cover and ferment on the pulp for 3 days, stirring daily. Then strain off the solids and place the liquor in a demijohn under airlock. Agitate the jar twice daily for the next 2 days, then add the remaining 1 lb (450g) of sugar. Again agitate the jar until the sugar has dissolved, and top up with cold water. Ferment to dryness in a warm place, racking immediately the wine is stable, and adding 1 Campden tablet. At its best this is a long-term wine, maturing for up to 18 months in bulk, but it is quite pleasant as a younger wine if sweetened to taste a few days before bottling.

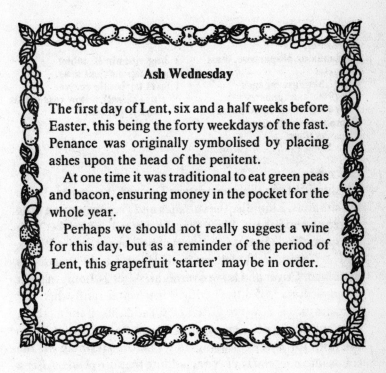

Ash Wednesday

The first day of Lent, six and a half weeks before Easter, this being the forty weekdays of the fast. Penance was originally symbolised by placing ashes upon the head of the penitent.

At one time it was traditional to eat green peas and bacon, ensuring money in the pocket for the whole year.

Perhaps we should not really suggest a wine for this day, but as a reminder of the period of Lent, this grapefruit 'starter' may be in order.

Greengage & Sultana

(a medium-dry, white table wine)

Ingredients

Bordeaux or all-purpose yeast
  starter
4 lb (1.8kg) greengages
2 lb (900g) sultanas
1 lb (450g) granulated sugar
Campden tablets as per
  instructions

1 3mg vitamin B₁ tablet
1 level tsp nutrient salts
1 level tsp pectic enzyme
½ pint (285ml) yellow rose petals
  (loosely packed)

Procedure

Wash and stone the greengages. Discard the stones. Wash
the sultanas. Liquidise the sultanas and greengages in a little
water or chop them. Place them in a sterilised bucket with
the sugar. Pour 5 pints (2.8 litres) of boiling water over them,
add 1 Campden tablet, and stir until all the sugar has
dissolved. Cover and leave overnight. After 24 hours make it
up to 8 pints (4.5 litres) with warm water, and when the
temperature is down to 70°F (21°C) add the vitamin tablet,
nutrient salts, pectic enzyme and yeast starter. Ferment on
the pulp for 3 days, stirring daily, before straining off the
solids into *a second bucket* and adding the rose petals. After a
further 2 days strain the liquor into a demijohn under airlock, and ferment to a finish in a warm place. Rack as soon as
the wine is stable, adding a Campden tablet, and rack a
second time within 4 weeks. Store in a cool place for the
maturation period. This wine could be drunk after 3–4
months.

May Day (1st May)

May Day celebrations were pre-Christian, and have their origin in the ancient Roman festival dedicated to Flora the Goddess of Flowers and Fruit. Appropriately, our wine for the day is a fruit wine.

On May Day, youths and maidens went out into the woods to find a birch or pine tree, which would be erected as a maypole in the village. A May Queen and May King or Green Man would be elected to reign, and a mock marriage would take place, though latterly only the May Queen seems to have been appointed for the day. The maypole would be garlanded with flowers, ribbons and may, and morris dancers would provide entertainment. This day was celebrated by rich and poor alike, and it was said that Henry VIII and the Royal Court took part. The most famous maypole was erected in the Strand in 1661, and was 134 feet high. It stood for 50 years, but those in the villages were usually taken down and used for building work. The present day maypole dancing is done by children holding ribbons and weaving patterns as they dance. This is a comparatively recent addition, and was introduced by John Ruskin from southern Europe about 100 years ago.

Another May Day survivor is the hobby horse, still brought out in Padstow and Minehead, each town having its own traditional ceremony.

Lemon Balm

(a light, delicate, medium-sweet table wine)

Ingredients

Champagne or all-purpose yeast
  starter
2 pints (1 litre) lemon balm
  leaves (with no stalks, loosely
  packed)
Campden tablet as per
  instructions
1 lb (450g) sultanas

1 26 fl oz (738ml) bottle of grape
  juice (N.B. containing no
  preservatives)
2¼ lb (1020g) granulated sugar
1 3mg vitamin B₁ tablet
½ level tsp citric acid
½ level tsp tartaric acid
1 level tsp pectic enzyme
1 level tsp nutrient salts

Procedure

Wash the lemon balm leaves in running water, and place
them in a sterilised bucket. Pour 4 pints (2 litres) of boiling
water over them, add 1 Campden tablet, cover, and leave for
48 hours, stirring twice daily. Then wash the sultanas.
Liquidise them in a little water or chop them. Add them, the
grape juice and the sugar to the bucket. Make it up to 1
gallon (4.5 litres) with hot water, stir until the sugar has
dissolved, and when the temperature is down to 70°F (21°C)
add the remaining ingredients, including the yeast starter.
Cover and ferment on the pulp for 3 days, stirring daily,
before straining off and placing the liquor into a demijohn
under airlock. Continue the fermentation to completion in a
warm place. Rack as soon as the wine is stable, and a second
time within 28 days. This wine could be drunk after 3
months.

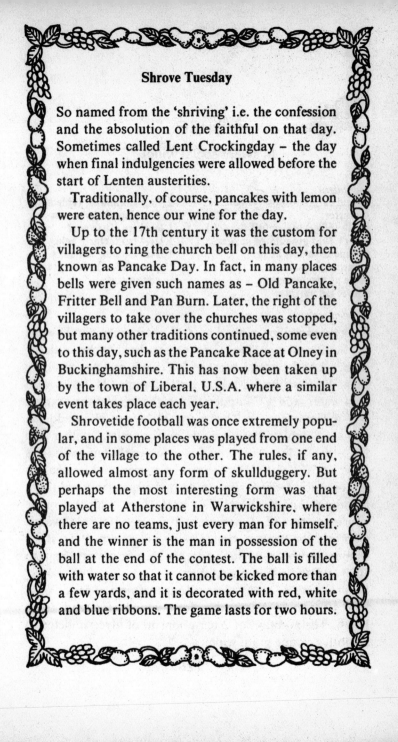

Shrove Tuesday

So named from the 'shriving' i.e. the confession and the absolution of the faithful on that day. Sometimes called Lent Crockingday – the day when final indulgencies were allowed before the start of Lenten austerities.

Traditionally, of course, pancakes with lemon were eaten, hence our wine for the day.

Up to the 17th century it was the custom for villagers to ring the church bell on this day, then known as Pancake Day. In fact, in many places bells were given such names as – Old Pancake, Fritter Bell and Pan Burn. Later, the right of the villagers to take over the churches was stopped, but many other traditions continued, some even to this day, such as the Pancake Race at Olney in Buckinghamshire. This has now been taken up by the town of Liberal, U.S.A. where a similar event takes place each year.

Shrovetide football was once extremely popular, and in some places was played from one end of the village to the other. The rules, if any, allowed almost any form of skullduggery. But perhaps the most interesting form was that played at Atherstone in Warwickshire, where there are no teams, just every man for himself, and the winner is the man in possession of the ball at the end of the contest. The ball is filled with water so that it cannot be kicked more than a few yards, and it is decorated with red, white and blue ribbons. The game lasts for two hours.

Maize

(a sweet social wine)

Ingredients

Cereal or all-purpose yeast
   starter
1½ lb (680g) maize (off the cob)
3 lb (1.4kg) granulated sugar
Campden tablets as per
   instructions
Juice of two oranges
1 level tsp amylase

2 3mg vitamin B_1 tablets
¼ level tsp grape tannin
1 level tsp citric acid
1 level tsp tartaric acid
1 level tsp nutrient salts
½ pint (285ml) white grape
   concentrate

Procedure

Soak the maize in 2 pints (1 litre) of water overnight. Discard
the liquid and place the maize in a sterilised bucket with the
sugar. Add 2 pints (1 litre) of hot water and stir until the
sugar has dissolved. Make it up to 5 pints (2.8 litres) with
cold water, add 1 Campden tablet, the juice of the oranges
and the amylase, and leave for 24 hours. Then add the
vitamin B_1 tablets, tannin, acids, nutrient salts, together with
2½ pints (1.4 litres) of warm water. When the temperature is
down to 70°F (21°C) add the yeast starter, and ferment on
the pulp for 4 days, stirring daily, before straining into a
demijohn under airlock. At this stage add the grape
concentrate, and if necessary top up with cold water.
Continue the fermentation to a finish in a warm place. If the
ferment is prolonged, rack once the specific gravity drops to
1020 and add a Campden tablet.

Note: as with all grain wines, a long maturation period of at
least 12 months is advisable, for a young wine tends to be
harsh. The addition of 2 teaspoonsful of glycerin helps to
smooth a young grain wine.

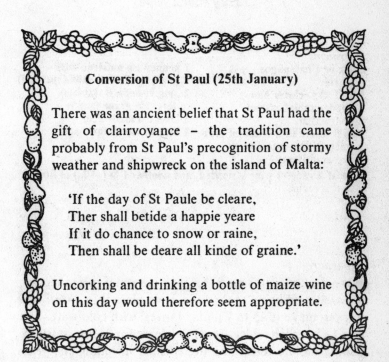

Conversion of St Paul (25th January)

There was an ancient belief that St Paul had the gift of clairvoyance – the tradition came probably from St Paul's precognition of stormy weather and shipwreck on the island of Malta:

'If the day of St Paule be cleare,
Ther shall betide a happie yeare
If it do chance to snow or raine,
Then shall be deare all kinde of graine.'

Uncorking and drinking a bottle of maize wine on this day would therefore seem appropriate.

Mead (Pyment)

(a dry social wine)

Ingredients

Hock or Champagne yeast
  starter
3 lb (1.4kg) clover honey
Campden tablets as per
  instructions
1 26 fl oz (738ml) bottle of grape
  juice (N.B. containing no
  preservatives)

1 heaped tsp nutrient salts
¼ level tsp Epsom salts (optional)
2 3mg vitamin B$_1$ tablets
¼ level tsp grape tannin
1 level tsp malic acid
1 heaped tsp tartaric acid

Note: if a sweeter wine is desired, add another 1 lb (450g) of honey
  to this recipe.

Procedure

Place the honey in 3 pints (1.7 litres) of water in a saucepan,
stir well, and bring to the boil. Then place it in a sterilised
bucket, make it up to 7 pints (4 litres) with cold water and
add 1 Campden tablet. Cover and leave for 24 hours, before
adding all the remaining ingredients, including the yeast
starter. Ferment in the bucket for 4 days, stirring daily,
before transferring to a demijohn under airlock. Ferment to
dryness in a warm place, then rack, add a Campden tablet
and top up with cold water. Allow to mature in a cool place,
giving the wine a second racking after about 3 months. This
is not a quick maturing wine, and will improve greatly with
keeping. If it is kept for a longer period, rack during
maturation at four monthly intervals.

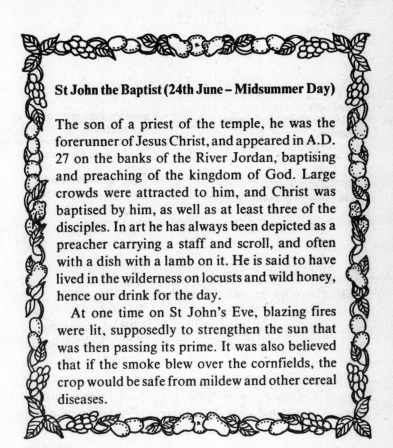

St John the Baptist (24th June – Midsummer Day)

The son of a priest of the temple, he was the forerunner of Jesus Christ, and appeared in A.D. 27 on the banks of the River Jordan, baptising and preaching of the kingdom of God. Large crowds were attracted to him, and Christ was baptised by him, as well as at least three of the disciples. In art he has always been depicted as a preacher carrying a staff and scroll, and often with a dish with a lamb on it. He is said to have lived in the wilderness on locusts and wild honey, hence our drink for the day.

At one time on St John's Eve, blazing fires were lit, supposedly to strengthen the sun that was then passing its prime. It was also believed that if the smoke blew over the cornfields, the crop would be safe from mildew and other cereal diseases.

Mint

(a light, dry table wine)

Ingredients

Chablis or all-purpose yeast
  starter
$1\frac{1}{2}$ pints (852ml) mint leaves
  (lightly bruised and loosely
  packed)
$\frac{1}{2}$ lb (227g) sultanas
$2\frac{1}{4}$ lb (1020g) granulated sugar

Campden tablets as per
  instructions
1 3mg vitamin B_1 tablet
$\frac{1}{2}$ level tsp grape tannin
1 heaped tsp citric acid
1 level tsp nutrient salts
1 level tsp pectic enzyme

Procedure

Wash the mint leaves thoroughly and place them in a sterilised bucket. Wash the sultanas. Liquidise them in a little water or chop them. Add them, with the sugar, to the bucket, together with 5 pints (2.8 litres) of boiling water. Add 1 Campden tablet, cover, and leave for 24 hours. Then add a further 3 pints (1.7 litres) of hot water, and when the temperature is down to 70°F (21°C) add the remaining ingredients, including the yeast starter. Ferment on the pulp for 3 days, stirring twice daily, and then strain the liquor into a *second sterilised bucket.* After a further 2 days, transfer to a demijohn under airlock, and ferment to a finish in a warm place. Rack as soon as possible once the wine is stable, adding a Campden tablet. A second racking will probably be required within 28 days. This wine could be drunk after 3–4 months.

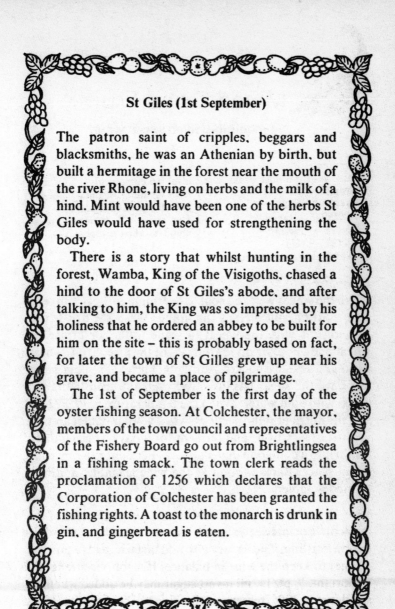

St Giles (1st September)

The patron saint of cripples, beggars and blacksmiths, he was an Athenian by birth, but built a hermitage in the forest near the mouth of the river Rhone, living on herbs and the milk of a hind. Mint would have been one of the herbs St Giles would have used for strengthening the body.

There is a story that whilst hunting in the forest, Wamba, King of the Visigoths, chased a hind to the door of St Giles's abode, and after talking to him, the King was so impressed by his holiness that he ordered an abbey to be built for him on the site – this is probably based on fact, for later the town of St Gilles grew up near his grave, and became a place of pilgrimage.

The 1st of September is the first day of the oyster fishing season. At Colchester, the mayor, members of the town council and representatives of the Fishery Board go out from Brightlingsea in a fishing smack. The town clerk reads the proclamation of 1256 which declares that the Corporation of Colchester has been granted the fishing rights. A toast to the monarch is drunk in gin, and gingerbread is eaten.

Mixed Dried Fruit

(a medium-bodied social wine)

Ingredients

Tokay or all-purpose yeast
   starter
1 lb (450g) wheat
1 lb (450g) sultanas
½ lb (227g) raisins
½ lb (227g) figs
2 lb (900g) granulated sugar

2 level tsp citric acid
1 level tsp nutrient salts
1 level tsp pectic enzyme
1 3mg vitamin B$_1$ tablet
Campden tablet as per
   instructions

Procedure

Wash the wheat well and soak it overnight in 1 pt (½ litre) of water. Strain and discard the liquid. Wash the dried fruit. Liquidise it with the wheat in some water, or bruise the wheat and chop the dried fruit. Place the dried fruit, wheat, sugar and acid in a bucket. Add 2 pts (1 litre) of boiling water. Stir until the sugar has dissolved. Make it up to 8 pts (4.5 litres) with cold water. When the temperature is 70°F/21°C add the nutrient salts, pectic enzyme, vitamin tablet and the yeast starter. Cover, and ferment for 5 days, stirring daily. Strain into a demijohn under airlock. Ferment to a finish in a warm place. Rack as soon as the wine is stable, adding 1 Campden tablet.

Note: this wine should be medium to dry at the end of the ferment. For a sweeter wine, sweeten to taste a few days before bottling; if necessary also add tartaric acid (a pinch at a time) to keep the wine in balance. If alcoholic strength is important, ¼ pt/142ml invert sugar may be added when the s.g. drops to 1006; remember the wine will become sweeter as the alcohol content rises. It may be drunk after 4–6 months.

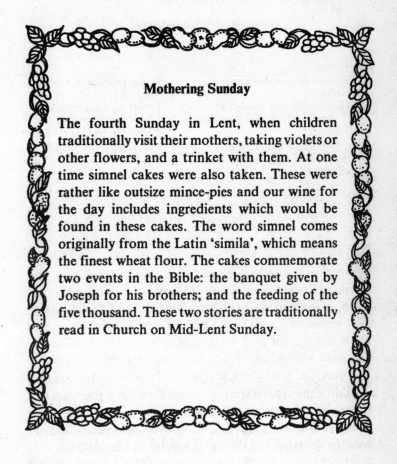

Mothering Sunday

The fourth Sunday in Lent, when children traditionally visit their mothers, taking violets or other flowers, and a trinket with them. At one time simnel cakes were also taken. These were rather like outsize mince-pies and our wine for the day includes ingredients which would be found in these cakes. The word simnel comes originally from the Latin 'simila', which means the finest wheat flour. The cakes commemorate two events in the Bible: the banquet given by Joseph for his brothers; and the feeding of the five thousand. These two stories are traditionally read in Church on Mid-Lent Sunday.

Oak Leaf

(a light, dry table wine)

Ingredients

Chablis or all-purpose yeast
   starter
1 gallon (4.5 litres) young oak
   leaves (loosely dropped into the
   container)
2 lb (900g) granulated sugar
8 fl oz (227ml) white grape
   concentrate

2 3mg vitamin B₁ tablets
Juice of 1 orange
1 level tsp tartaric acid
1 level tsp citric acid
1 level tsp pectic enzyme
1 level tsp nutrient salts

Procedure

Wash the oak leaves in cold water and place them in a
sterilised bucket. Pour 4 pints (2 litres) of boiling water over
them, cover, and leave for 24 hours. Strain off the liquid into
a *second bucket*, add the sugar and a further 2 pints (1 litre) of
hot water and stir until the sugar has dissolved. Make it up to
8 pints (4.5 litres) with cold water, and when the temperature
is down to 70°F (21°C) add the remaining ingredients,
including the yeast starter. Ferment for 4 days, stirring daily,
before transferring to a demijohn under airlock. Top up as
necessary, and ferment to a finish in a warm place. Rack as
soon as the wine is stable, and mature in a cool place.
Note: the addition of 2 tsp of glycerin added to the demijohn
before bottling, i.e. during the maturation period, will
improve this wine. The wine could be drunk after 3–4
months.

Arbor Day (29th May)

Proclaimed by King Charles II to commemorate his escape when he hid in the oak tree after the Battle of Worcester, this day has become known as Oak Apple Day. Charles II founded the Royal Hospital at Chelsea – the Home for Retired Soldiers (known as the Chelsea Pensioners) – and on this day the Pensioners parade, and are inspected, often by a member of the Royal family. All wear oak leaf buttonholes, and the statue of King Charles is also decorated. The celebrations include plum pudding and extra beer for the old men.

Orange

(a medium or sweet table wine)

Ingredients

Sauternes or all-purpose yeast starter
12 sweet medium-sized oranges
2½ lb (1.1kg) granulated sugar
1 3mg vitamin B₁ tablet
1 level tsp pectic enzyme
1 level tsp nutrient salts
Campden tablet as per instructions

Procedure

Wash the oranges and peel 6 of them thinly, carefully avoiding the white pith. Place the sugar in a sterilised bucket and pour in 3 pints (1.7 litres) of boiling water. Stir until the sugar has dissolved, and then add the peel of the 6 oranges. Cover and leave overnight, and then add the juice from all 12 oranges. Make it up to 8 pints (4.5 litres) with warm water, and when the temperature is down to 70°F (21°C) add the remaining ingredients, including the yeast starter. Ferment for 5 days, stirring daily, before straining into a demijohn under airlock. Ferment to completion in a warm place. Rack as soon as the wine is stable, adding 1 Campden tablet, and rack a second time within 28 days. Sweeten to taste a few days before bottling, but watch the acidity, it may be necessary to add a little acid to balance the sugar. This wine could be drunk after 4 months.

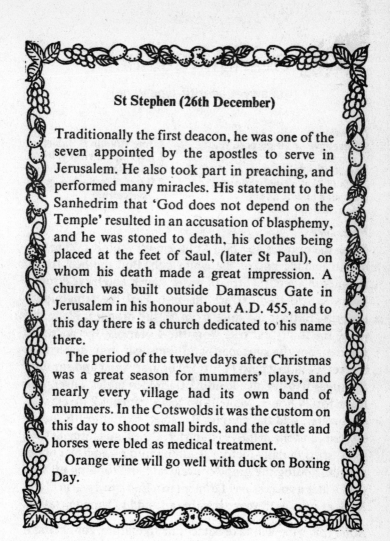

St Stephen (26th December)

Traditionally the first deacon, he was one of the seven appointed by the apostles to serve in Jerusalem. He also took part in preaching, and performed many miracles. His statement to the Sanhedrim that 'God does not depend on the Temple' resulted in an accusation of blasphemy, and he was stoned to death, his clothes being placed at the feet of Saul, (later St Paul), on whom his death made a great impression. A church was built outside Damascus Gate in Jerusalem in his honour about A.D. 455, and to this day there is a church dedicated to his name there.

The period of the twelve days after Christmas was a great season for mummers' plays, and nearly every village had its own band of mummers. In the Cotswolds it was the custom on this day to shoot small birds, and the cattle and horses were bled as medical treatment.

Orange wine will go well with duck on Boxing Day.

Orange (Seville)

(a sweet aperitif-type wine)

Ingredients

Champagne or all-purpose yeast
  starter
8 small Seville oranges
2½ lb (1.1kg) granulated sugar
Campden tablets as per
  instructions

1 3mg vitamin B₁ tablet
1 level tsp nutrient salts
1 level tsp pectic enzyme
8 fl oz (227ml) white grape
  concentrate

Procedure

Wash the oranges and peel 4 of them very thinly taking care
not to include any of the white pith. Boil the peel for 20
minutes in a pint (½ litre) of water, cover, and leave it for 24
hours in order to extract the zest. Peel the remaining 4
oranges. Extract the juice from all the oranges. Place this
juice, the thinly cut peel from the 4 oranges, the juice and
water (from the saucepan) and the sugar, into a sterilised
bucket. Pour in 2 pints (1 litre) of boiling water and stir until
the sugar has dissolved. Add 1 Campden tablet, cover, and
leave for 24 hours. Make it up to 7½ pints (4.2 litres) with
cold water, add the vitamin B₁ tablet, nutrient salts, pectic
enzyme, and stir in the yeast starter. Cover, and ferment for 4
days, stirring daily, before straining into a demijohn under
airlock, adding the grape concentrate and topping up with
cold water as necessary. Ferment to a finish in a warm place.
Rack as soon as the wine is stable and add 1 Campden tablet.

Note: this wine will take some time to mature, for at first it
will be inclined to be bitter. Time will mellow this, and when
it is finally ready (probably after 6 months) it can be
sweetened to taste.

138

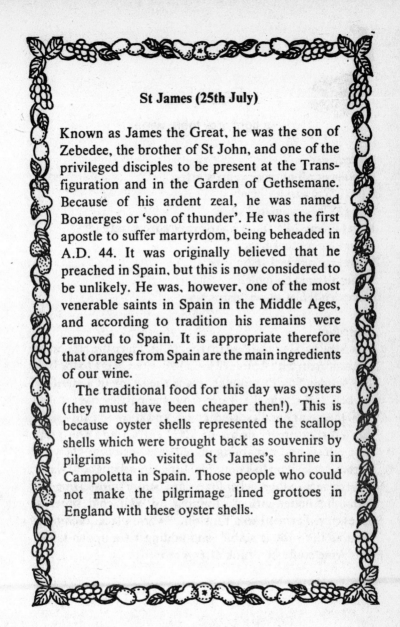

St James (25th July)

Known as James the Great, he was the son of Zebedee, the brother of St John, and one of the privileged disciples to be present at the Transfiguration and in the Garden of Gethsemane. Because of his ardent zeal, he was named Boanerges or 'son of thunder'. He was the first apostle to suffer martyrdom, being beheaded in A.D. 44. It was originally believed that he preached in Spain, but this is now considered to be unlikely. He was, however, one of the most venerable saints in Spain in the Middle Ages, and according to tradition his remains were removed to Spain. It is appropriate therefore that oranges from Spain are the main ingredients of our wine.

The traditional food for this day was oysters (they must have been cheaper then!). This is because oyster shells represented the scallop shells which were brought back as souvenirs by pilgrims who visited St James's shrine in Campoletta in Spain. Those people who could not make the pilgrimage lined grottoes in England with these oyster shells.

Parsley

(a light, dry table wine)

Ingredients
Chablis or all-purpose yeast starter
8 oz (227g) parsley heads
8 oz (227g) granulated sugar
1 tin (700ml/24½ fl oz) white grape concentrate (dry)
1 level tsp pectic enzyme
1 level tsp nutrient salts
1 3mg vitamin B₁ tablet
Campden tablet as per instructions

Procedure
Wash the parsley and discard the stalks. Place the remainder
in a saucepan with 4 pints (2 litres) of water, bring to the boil,
and simmer for 15 minutes. Place the sugar in a sterilised
bucket, and strain the water from the parsley over it. Stir
until the sugar has dissolved, cover, and allow to cool – when
the temperature is down to 70°F (21°C) add the grape
concentrate and remaining ingredients, including the yeast
starter. Make it up to 8 pints (4.5 litres) by adding cold water,
and ferment in the bucket for 5 days before transferring to a
demijohn under airlock, topping up with cold water as
necessary. Ferment to a finish in a warm place, racking as
soon as the wine is stable, and adding 1 Campden tablet.
This wine could be drunk after 4 months.

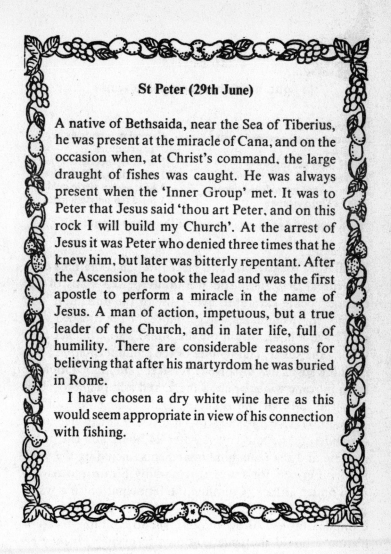

St Peter (29th June)

A native of Bethsaida, near the Sea of Tiberius, he was present at the miracle of Cana, and on the occasion when, at Christ's command, the large draught of fishes was caught. He was always present when the 'Inner Group' met. It was to Peter that Jesus said 'thou art Peter, and on this rock I will build my Church'. At the arrest of Jesus it was Peter who denied three times that he knew him, but later was bitterly repentant. After the Ascension he took the lead and was the first apostle to perform a miracle in the name of Jesus. A man of action, impetuous, but a true leader of the Church, and in later life, full of humility. There are considerable reasons for believing that after his martyrdom he was buried in Rome.

I have chosen a dry white wine here as this would seem appropriate in view of his connection with fishing.

Parsnip

(a light, medium-sweet table wine)

Ingredients

Sauternes or all-purpose yeast
  starter
4 lb (1.8kg) parsnips
2 oranges
2½ lb (1.1kg) granulated sugar
½ lb (227g) sultanas

Campden tablets as per
  instructions
1 level tsp pectic enzyme
1 3mg vitamin B₁ tablet
1 heaped tsp citric acid
1 level tsp nutrient salts

This is best made towards the end of the winter months.

Procedure

Scrub, slice the parsnips and place in a pan containing 6 pts
(3.4 litres) of water. Add the thinly peeled skins of the
oranges, being careful to avoid any of the pith. Boil, and
simmer for 10 minutes – never more, or the finished wine
may have a haze. Strain off the liquid into a bucket containing the sugar, taking note of the amount of liquid. Stir
until the sugar has dissolved. Wash the sultanas. Liquidise
them in some water or chop them, and add them, together
with the juice of the oranges, again taking note of the
amount. Make it up to 8 pts (4.5 litres) with cold water, add 1
Campden tablet and cover. After 24 hours add the pectic
enzyme and the remaining ingredients, including the yeast
starter. Ferment for 4 days, stirring daily. Strain into a demijohn under airlock. Continue the fermentation in a warm
place until the s.g. is down to 1006, then rack and add 1
Campden tablet. Allow the ferment to continue to completion. Should the wine go down to dryness, it may be
sweetened a few days before bottling. This wine may be
drunk after 6 months.

Harvest

A time of thanksgiving for the fruits of the earth. In many churches it is usual for congregations to decorate their churches with fruits, flowers and vegetables including parsnips, which are later donated to charity.

The age old rites of the corn harvest go back to ancient Greece, and have been kept in some parts until quite recently. When harvesting the fields, the men would work in steadily decreasing circles until only the final ears were left. It was thought that the 'Corn Spirit' hid in these ears and as no man wanted to be branded a 'Spirit Captor', each man would throw a sickle at the ears from a safe distance. The last five stalks were then made into a corn dolly and kept. It was also customary for anyone passing a body of reapers in harvest time to shout 'forther thee', to which the response was 'thank ye'. This was probably based on the Book of Ruth "and behold, Boaz came from Bethlehem and said to the reapers, 'the Lord be with you', and they answered him, 'the Lord bless thee'".

One family in Northumberland has for over a hundred years made a corn baby, the height of a sheaf of corn, which is left in the church until the next year.

Peach

(a sweet, white table wine)

Ingredients

Tokay or Sauternes yeast starter
2¼ lb (1020g) granulated sugar
1 15 oz (425g) tin peaches
(N.B. containing no preservatives)
1 3mg vitamin B₁ tablet
½ level tsp grape tannin
2 level tsp pectic enzyme

1 heaped tsp citric acid
1 level tsp tartaric acid
1 level tsp nutrient salts
8 fl oz (227ml) white grape
  concentrate
Campden tablet as per
  instructions

Procedure

Place the sugar in a sterilised bucket and pour on 3 pints
(1.7 litres) of hot water. Stir until the sugar has dissolved, then
add the peaches, chopping them as small as possible. Make it
up to 7½ pints (4.2 litres) with cold water, and when the
temperature is down to 70°F (21°C) add all the ingredients
except the grape concentrate. Ferment on the pulp for 4
days, stirring daily, then strain the fermenting must into a
demijohn under airlock, adding the concentrate and topping
up as necessary. Ferment to a finish in a warm place, racking
as soon as the wine is stable and adding 1 Campden tablet.
Rack again within 28 days. This wine may well go down to
dryness, and once it is stable, it should then be sweetened to
taste – probably to about 1024 s.g. The wine could be drunk
after 3–4 months.

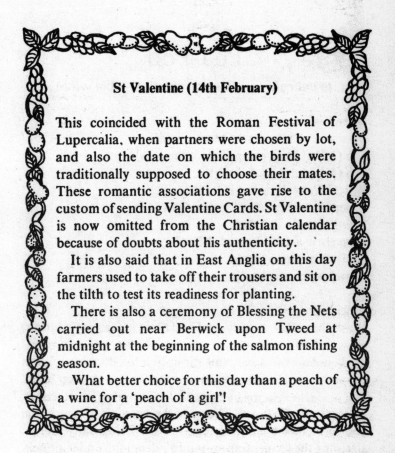

St Valentine (14th February)

This coincided with the Roman Festival of Lupercalia, when partners were chosen by lot, and also the date on which the birds were traditionally supposed to choose their mates. These romantic associations gave rise to the custom of sending Valentine Cards. St Valentine is now omitted from the Christian calendar because of doubts about his authenticity.

It is also said that in East Anglia on this day farmers used to take off their trousers and sit on the tilth to test its readiness for planting.

There is also a ceremony of Blessing the Nets carried out near Berwick upon Tweed at midnight at the beginning of the salmon fishing season.

What better choice for this day than a peach of a wine for a 'peach of a girl'!

Pea-Pod

(a delicate, medium-sweet, light table wine)

Ingredients
Bordeaux or all-purpose yeast starter
5 lb (2.3kg) fresh pea-pods (not the peas)
3 lb (1.4kg) granulated sugar
½ lb (227g) sultanas
Campden tablets as per instructions
1 3mg vitamin B₁ tablet
2 tsp citric acid (1 heaped, 1 level)
½ level tsp grape tannin
1 level tsp nutrient salts

Procedure
Wash the pods carefully, and boil them in 6 pints (3.4 litres)
of water until tender, then strain the liquor into a sterilised
bucket. Add the sugar, and stir until it has dissolved. Wash
the sultanas. Liquidise them in a little water or chop them,
and place them in the bucket. Add 1 Campden tablet, cover,
and leave for 24 hours. Then add the remaining ingredients,
and ferment on the pulp for 3 days, stirring daily, before
straining the fermenting must into a demijohn under airlock.
Make it up to 8 pints (4.5 litres) by adding cold water as soon
as the heavy ferment subsides. Ferment to a finish in a warm
place, adding a Campden tablet at the first and second
rackings. This wine could be drunk after 3–4 months.

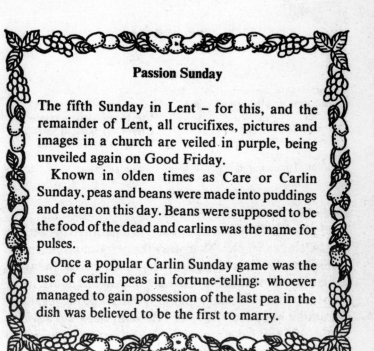

Passion Sunday

The fifth Sunday in Lent – for this, and the remainder of Lent, all crucifixes, pictures and images in a church are veiled in purple, being unveiled again on Good Friday.

Known in olden times as Care or Carlin Sunday, peas and beans were made into puddings and eaten on this day. Beans were supposed to be the food of the dead and carlins was the name for pulses.

Once a popular Carlin Sunday game was the use of carlin peas in fortune-telling: whoever managed to gain possession of the last pea in the dish was believed to be the first to marry.

Pear

(a light table wine, best medium-sweet)

Ingredients

Champagne or all-purpose yeast
  starter
Campden tablets as per
  instructions
4 lb (1.8kg) pears
2 lb (900g) granulated sugar

1 3mg vitamin B_1 tablet
1 level tsp pectic enzyme
1 level tsp nutrient salts
1 heaped tsp citric acid
8 fl oz (227ml) white grape
  concentrate

Procedure

Put 3 pints (1.7 litres) of tepid water in a sterilised bucket and add 1 Campden tablet. Then wash the pears, chop, and place them immediately into the bucket. (This is in order to avoid oxidation.) Cover and leave overnight. After 24 hours, make it up to 6 pints (3.4 litres) with warm water, add the sugar and stir until it has dissolved. When the temperature is down to 70°F (21°C) add the remaining ingredients (including the yeast starter) with the exception of the grape concentrate, and ferment on the pulp for 3 days, stirring daily. Then strain the fermenting must into a demijohn under airlock, and after a further 2 days, add the grape concentrate and make it up to 1 gallon (4.5 litres) with cold water. Ferment to a finish in a warm place, and rack as soon as the wine is stable, adding 1 Campden tablet. Rack a second time within 21 days. The wine may be sweetened to taste a few days before bottling and it may be necessary to adjust the acid level if the pears used were very ripe. The wine could be drunk after 3–4 months.

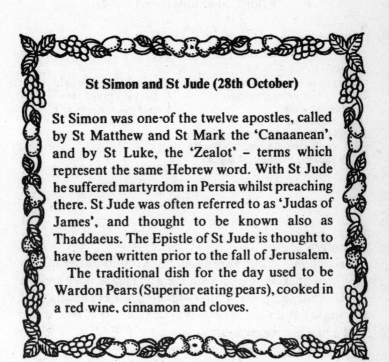

St Simon and St Jude (28th October)

St Simon was one of the twelve apostles, called by St Matthew and St Mark the 'Canaanean', and by St Luke, the 'Zealot' – terms which represent the same Hebrew word. With St Jude he suffered martyrdom in Persia whilst preaching there. St Jude was often referred to as 'Judas of James', and thought to be known also as Thaddaeus. The Epistle of St Jude is thought to have been written prior to the fall of Jerusalem.

The traditional dish for the day used to be Wardon Pears (Superior eating pears), cooked in a red wine, cinnamon and cloves.

Pineapple & Grape

(a light, medium-sweet wine)

Ingredients

Champagne yeast starter
2 15 oz (435g) tins pineapple in
   syrup, or pulp
(N.B. containing no preservatives)
2 pints (1 litre) white grape juice
(N.B. containing no preservatives)
2¼ lb (1020g) granulated sugar

1 heaped tsp citric acid
½ level tsp grape tannin
1 level tsp nutrient salts
1 level tsp pectic enzyme

Procedure

Finely chop the pineapple and place it and its syrup in a sterilised bucket together with the white grape juice and the sugar. Pour in 2 pints (1 litre) of boiling water and stir until the sugar has dissolved. Add 4 pints (2 litres) of cold water and when the temperature is down to 70°F (21°C) add the remaining ingredients, including the yeast starter. Cover, and ferment on the pulp for 3 days, stirring daily, before straining the must into a demijohn under airlock, topping up with cold water if necessary. Continue the fermentation in a warm place, racking as soon as the wine is stable. This wine will be drinkable in 3 months, but will improve if kept a little longer.

Note: for a heavier wine, add another tin of pineapple and a further 1 lb (450g) of sugar.

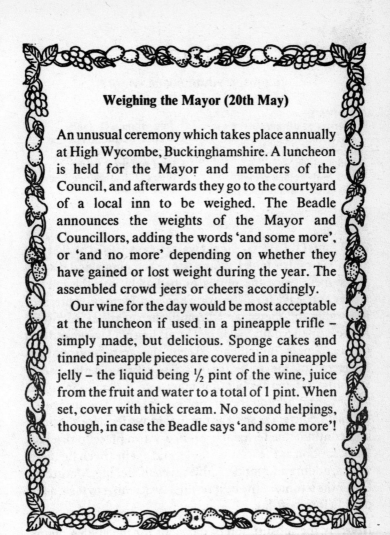

Weighing the Mayor (20th May)

An unusual ceremony which takes place annually at High Wycombe, Buckinghamshire. A luncheon is held for the Mayor and members of the Council, and afterwards they go to the courtyard of a local inn to be weighed. The Beadle announces the weights of the Mayor and Councillors, adding the words 'and some more', or 'and no more' depending on whether they have gained or lost weight during the year. The assembled crowd jeers or cheers accordingly.

Our wine for the day would be most acceptable at the luncheon if used in a pineapple trifle – simply made, but delicious. Sponge cakes and tinned pineapple pieces are covered in a pineapple jelly – the liquid being $\frac{1}{2}$ pint of the wine, juice from the fruit and water to a total of 1 pint. When set, cover with thick cream. No second helpings, though, in case the Beadle says 'and some more'!

Plum

(a sweet, white social wine)

Ingredients

Sauternes or all-purpose yeast
  starter
Campden tablets as per
  instructions
4 lb (1.8kg) golden plums
2½ lb (1.1kg) granulated sugar

1 3mg vitamin B₁ tablet
1 heaped tsp pectic enzyme
1 level tsp nutrient salts
1 level tsp citric acid
8 fl oz (227ml) white grape
  concentrate

Procedure

Put 3 pints (1.7 litres) of tepid water in a sterilised bucket and
add 1 Campden tablet. Wash, stone the plums and discard
the stones. Place the plums immediately into the bucket.
Cover and leave for 24 hours. Then add 3 pints (1.7 litres) of
hot water and the sugar. Stir until the sugar has dissolved.
Make it up to 6 pints (3.4 litres) by adding cold water and add
the remaining ingredients except the grape concentrate.
Ferment on the pulp for 4 days, stirring daily, before
straining off the fermenting must into a demijohn under
airlock, and adding the grape concentrate. Top up with 1
gallon (4.5 litres) as soon as the first heavy ferment subsides,
and continue the fermentation in a warm place to dryness.
Rack as soon as the wine is stable, and again after a further 3
weeks, adding a Campden tablet at each racking. Mature for
6 months to obtain the best results, sweetening to taste a few
days before bottling.

Note: by the substitution of damsons for the golden plums,
and red concentrate for white, a rich sweet red social wine
can be made.

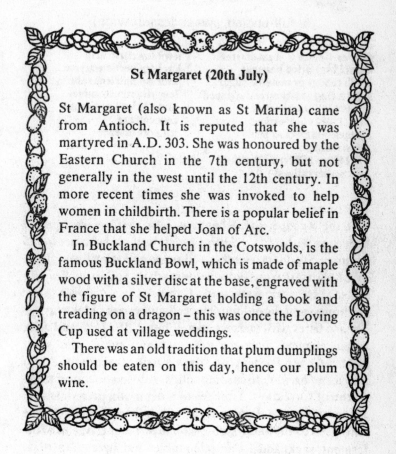

St Margaret (20th July)

St Margaret (also known as St Marina) came from Antioch. It is reputed that she was martyred in A.D. 303. She was honoured by the Eastern Church in the 7th century, but not generally in the west until the 12th century. In more recent times she was invoked to help women in childbirth. There is a popular belief in France that she helped Joan of Arc.

In Buckland Church in the Cotswolds, is the famous Buckland Bowl, which is made of maple wood with a silver disc at the base, engraved with the figure of St Margaret holding a book and treading on a dragon – this was once the Loving Cup used at village weddings.

There was an old tradition that plum dumplings should be eaten on this day, hence our plum wine.

Port-type

(a full-bodied, sweet dessert wine)

Ingredients

Port or Gervin 6 yeast starter
4 oz (114g) dried bananas
1½ lb (680g) granulated sugar
3 lb (1.4kg) elderberries, stripped
2 lb (900g) blackberries
4 oz (114g) raspberries
Campden tablets as per
   instructions
1 lb (450g) bilberries (bottled –
   no preservatives)

1 level tsp citric acid
1 level tsp pectic enzyme
1 level tsp nutrient salts
1 3mg vitamin B₁ tablet
½ pint (285ml) red grape
   concentrate
2 dsp port essence
Invert sugar as required

Procedure

Cut the washed, dried bananas into small pieces, put in saucepan with 3 pts/1.7 litres water, boil, and simmer for 25 minutes. Strain into bucket add sugar and stir till dissolved. Wash the fresh fruit; liquidise or mash it. Add to bucket with 2 pts/1 litre warm water and a Campden tablet; cover. After 24 hours add liquidised/mashed bilberries. Make up to 7 pts/4 litres with warm water. When 70°F/21°C add acid, pectic enzyme, nutrient salts, vitamin tablet and yeast starter. Cover, ferment for 3 days, stirring twice daily. Strain into a *2nd bucket*, discarding solids. Add grape concentrate. Ferment for 2 days. Transfer to a demijohn under airlock. Add port essence. Top up at end of heavy ferment. Each time s.g. drops to 1006 add ¼ pt/142ml invert sugar. At end of the ferment, rack, add 1 Campden tablet and sweeten to 1026. Rack again after 28 days and again 2 months later. To be at its best, keep for at least 12 months, adding a small amount of brandy to taste.

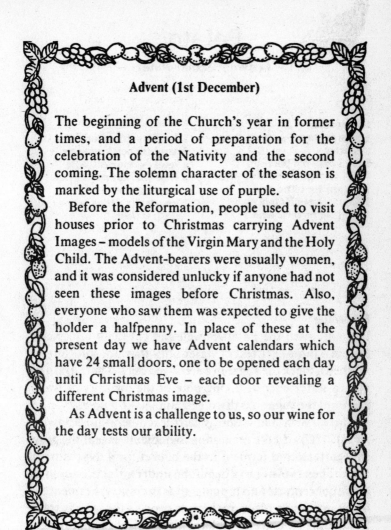

Advent (1st December)

The beginning of the Church's year in former times, and a period of preparation for the celebration of the Nativity and the second coming. The solemn character of the season is marked by the liturgical use of purple.

Before the Reformation, people used to visit houses prior to Christmas carrying Advent Images – models of the Virgin Mary and the Holy Child. The Advent-bearers were usually women, and it was considered unlucky if anyone had not seen these images before Christmas. Also, everyone who saw them was expected to give the holder a halfpenny. In place of these at the present day we have Advent calendars which have 24 small doors, one to be opened each day until Christmas Eve – each door revealing a different Christmas image.

As Advent is a challenge to us, so our wine for the day tests our ability.

Potato

(a sweet social wine)

Ingredients

Sauternes or all-purpose yeast
   starter
5 lb (2.3kg) old potatoes
3½ lb (1.6kg) granulated sugar
1 heaped tsp citric acid
3 3mg vitamin B₁ tablets
1 level tsp tartaric acid

1 level tsp grape tannin
1 level tsp pectic enzyme
1 level tsp nutrient salts
8 fl oz (227ml) white grape
   concentrate
Campden tablet as per
   instructions

Procedure

Peel and wash the potatoes well and cut them into pieces.
Boil in 4 pints (2 litres) of water until they are soft (but not
mashed). Place the sugar in a sterilised bucket and strain the
potato water over it, taking note of the quantity of water.
Stir until the sugar has dissolved, and make it up to 7½ pints
(4.2 litres) with cold water. When the temperature is down to
70°F (21°C) add the remaining ingredients except the grape
concentrate, and ferment in the bucket for 4 days, stirring
daily. Then transfer to a demijohn under airlock, adding the
grape concentrate and topping up as necessary. Ferment to a
finish in a warm place, racking as soon as the wine is stable
and adding 1 Campden tablet. This wine is slow-maturing so
if possible leave in bulk for at least 12 months before
sweetening to taste and bottling.

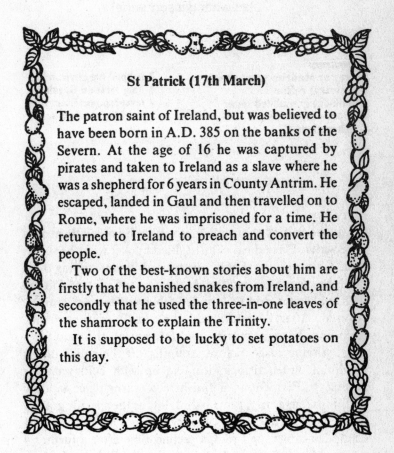

St Patrick (17th March)

The patron saint of Ireland, but was believed to have been born in A.D. 385 on the banks of the Severn. At the age of 16 he was captured by pirates and taken to Ireland as a slave where he was a shepherd for 6 years in County Antrim. He escaped, landed in Gaul and then travelled on to Rome, where he was imprisoned for a time. He returned to Ireland to preach and convert the people.

Two of the best-known stories about him are firstly that he banished snakes from Ireland, and secondly that he used the three-in-one leaves of the shamrock to explain the Trinity.

It is supposed to be lucky to set potatoes on this day.

Raisin

(a sweet dessert wine)

Ingredients

Sherry or Madeira yeast starter
3 lb (1.4kg) raisins
1 lb (450g) granulated sugar
Campden tablets as per
  instructions

1 heaped tsp citric acid
1 3mg vitamin B$_1$ tablet
1 level tsp pectic enzyme
1 level tsp nutrient salts

Procedure

Wash the raisins thoroughly, chop or liquidise them in a little water. Place them in a sterilised bucket with the sugar. Pour 4 pints (2 litres) of hot water over them, stirring them until the sugar has dissolved. Make it up to 8 pints (4.5 litres) with cold water, add 1 Campden tablet and leave overnight, covered. After 24 hours add the remaining ingredients, including the yeast starter, and ferment on the pulp for 5 days, stirring daily, before straining off the solids into a demijohn under airlock, topping up with cold water as necessary. Ferment to a finish in a warm place, adding additional sugar in ¼ pint (142ml) lots as the specific gravity drops to 1006. Rack as soon as the wine is stable, adding 1 Campden tablet, and rack a second time after a further 4 weeks. Mature in a cool place in the demijohn as long as possible as this will greatly improve the wine. It could be drunk after 4–6 months.

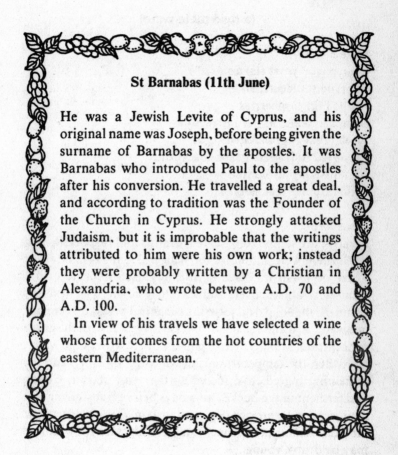

St Barnabas (11th June)

He was a Jewish Levite of Cyprus, and his original name was Joseph, before being given the surname of Barnabas by the apostles. It was Barnabas who introduced Paul to the apostles after his conversion. He travelled a great deal, and according to tradition was the Founder of the Church in Cyprus. He strongly attacked Judaism, but it is improbable that the writings attributed to him were his own work; instead they were probably written by a Christian in Alexandria, who wrote between A.D. 70 and A.D. 100.

In view of his travels we have selected a wine whose fruit comes from the hot countries of the eastern Mediterranean.

Redcurrant

(a rosé table wine)

Ingredients
Champagne yeast starter
2 lb (900g) redcurrants
4 oz (114g) raspberries
Campden tablet as per instructions
2¼ lb (1020g) granulated sugar
8 fl oz (227ml) white grape concentrate
1 level tsp pectic enzyme
1 level tsp nutrient salts

Procedure
Remove the stems from the redcurrants and raspberries and wash them well. Liquidise the fruit in 3 pints (1.7 litres) of water or mash it. Place it in a sterilised bucket. Add 1 Campden tablet, cover, and leave overnight. The next day strain off the solids, dissolve the sugar in 3 pints (1.7 litres) of hot water and add this to the bucket, together with the grape concentrate. Make it up to 8 pints (4.5 litres) with cold water, and when the temperature is down to 70°F (21°C) add the remaining ingredients, including the yeast starter. Cover, and ferment in the bucket for 5 days before transferring to a demijohn under airlock. Ferment to a finish in a warm place, racking as soon as the wine is stable. This is a light wine and may be drunk young.

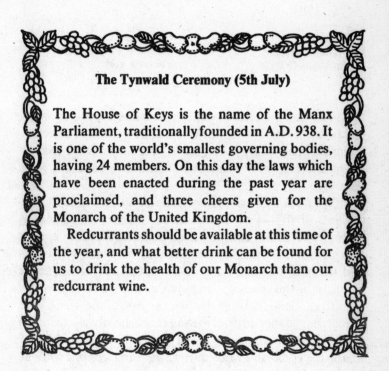

The Tynwald Ceremony (5th July)

The House of Keys is the name of the Manx Parliament, traditionally founded in A.D. 938. It is one of the world's smallest governing bodies, having 24 members. On this day the laws which have been enacted during the past year are proclaimed, and three cheers given for the Monarch of the United Kingdom.

Redcurrants should be available at this time of the year, and what better drink can be found for us to drink the health of our Monarch than our redcurrant wine.

Reverendine

(a delicious golden liqueur)

Ingredients

A golden wine
Reverendine essence
Caster sugar to taste

Glycerin
Vodka or Polish spirit
Tartaric acid

Procedure

Note that the quantities of the ingredients are not shown – this is deliberate, for so much depends on the wine selected. It should be as strong in alcohol as possible (in order to keep down the cost of vodka) but should not have a strong flavour.

Take an empty sterilised bottle and pour in about 13 fl oz (390ml) of the wine. To this, add 2 tsp of Reverendine essence and shake until it is well blended. Taste to ensure that the original wine flavour has been completely overcome and the herb flavour is correct, if not add a further small quantity of the essence. Then add caster sugar (again the quantity depends entirely on the sweetness of the wine base). Shake thoroughly until all the sugar has dissolved – taste for sweetness. Add about 1½ tsp of glycerin to add body, and finally the vodka or Polish spirit to gain an alcoholic content of about 56 proof. Here you will need to use the Pearson Square (see page 41) to assess the quantity. Again taste, for it is likely that in blending and sweetening, the liqueur may need the addition of a pinch or two of tartaric acid to balance it. Shake the bottle well to assist in blending; it may be drunk at once, but obviously improves greatly if allowed to blend and mature naturally.

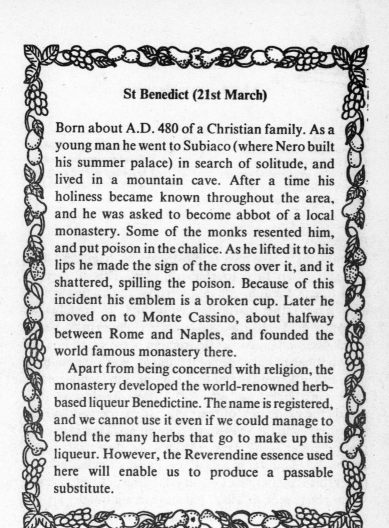

St Benedict (21st March)

Born about A.D. 480 of a Christian family. As a young man he went to Subiaco (where Nero built his summer palace) in search of solitude, and lived in a mountain cave. After a time his holiness became known throughout the area, and he was asked to become abbot of a local monastery. Some of the monks resented him, and put poison in the chalice. As he lifted it to his lips he made the sign of the cross over it, and it shattered, spilling the poison. Because of this incident his emblem is a broken cup. Later he moved on to Monte Cassino, about halfway between Rome and Naples, and founded the world famous monastery there.

Apart from being concerned with religion, the monastery developed the world-renowned herb-based liqueur Benedictine. The name is registered, and we cannot use it even if we could manage to blend the many herbs that go to make up this liqueur. However, the Reverendine essence used here will enable us to produce a passable substitute.

Rhubarb

(a light, dry table wine)

Ingredients
Champagne yeast starter
4 lb (1.8kg) rhubarb
2 lb (900g) granulated sugar
2 pints (1 litre) grape juice
(N.B. containing no preservatives)

1 3mg vitamin B$_1$ tablet
$\frac{1}{2}$ level tsp grape tannin
1 level tsp pectic enzyme
1 level tsp nutrient salts

Procedure
Probably as it is grown in most gardens, beginners' first thoughts often turn to rhubarb wine. This is perhaps unfortunate, for although rhubarb does make a fine wine, it does have rather particular difficulties. It contains an unwanted acid known as oxalic acid in globules in the sticks, which occasionally causes destruction of the yeast. For this reason it has to have special treatment. Wash the rhubarb well, slice it longways and then cut into 2 in (5cm) lengths. Place it in a bucket, add 6$\frac{1}{2}$ pts (3.7 litres) of *cold* water (this avoids the extraction of the oxalic acid), then add all the ingredients and the yeast starter, cover, and keep in a warm place. Ferment for 2 days, stirring daily, then strain into a *2nd* bucket. Transfer to a demijohn under airlock as soon as this ferment is complete (4–5 days), Ferment to a finish in a warm place, rack as usual, but store in a jar under airlock as this wine does sometimes have what is known as a 'malolactic ferment'. This, which is rather like a secondary ferment, occurs when ingredients containing large amounts of malic acid (such as rhubarb) are used. The wine may be drunk after 4 months.

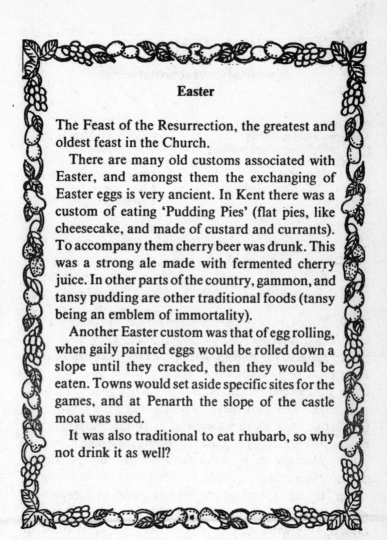

Easter

The Feast of the Resurrection, the greatest and oldest feast in the Church.

There are many old customs associated with Easter, and amongst them the exchanging of Easter eggs is very ancient. In Kent there was a custom of eating 'Pudding Pies' (flat pies, like cheesecake, and made of custard and currants). To accompany them cherry beer was drunk. This was a strong ale made with fermented cherry juice. In other parts of the country, gammon, and tansy pudding are other traditional foods (tansy being an emblem of immortality).

Another Easter custom was that of egg rolling, when gaily painted eggs would be rolled down a slope until they cracked, then they would be eaten. Towns would set aside specific sites for the games, and at Penarth the slope of the castle moat was used.

It was also traditional to eat rhubarb, so why not drink it as well?

Rice & Raisin

(a medium-sweet social wine)

Ingredients

All-purpose yeast starter
1¾ lb (800g) rice (short pudding rice)
1 lb (450g) raisins
2½ lb (1.1kg) granulated sugar
2 oranges

Campden tablets as per instructions
1 3mg vitamin B₁ tablet
2 level tsp citric acid
1 level tsp pectic enzyme
1 level tsp nutrient salts

Procedure

Wash the rice and raisins. Chop the raisins and place them in a sterilised bucket. Add the sugar, rice, juice and thinly peeled skins of the oranges, being careful to avoid the pith. Pour on 4 pints (2 litres) of boiling water, and stir until the sugar has dissolved. Then add 1 Campden tablet, cover, and leave overnight. After 24 hours make it up to 8 pints (4.5 litres) with warm water, and when the temperature is down to 70°F (21°C) add the remaining ingredients, including the yeast starter. Ferment on the pulp for 6 days, stirring daily, before straining the fermenting must into a demijohn under airlock. Continue the fermentation to completion, and rack as soon as the wine is stable and add a Campden tablet. This wine may be drunk very young if fined or filtered, but if it is to be kept, add 1 Campden tablet and store for about 9 months.

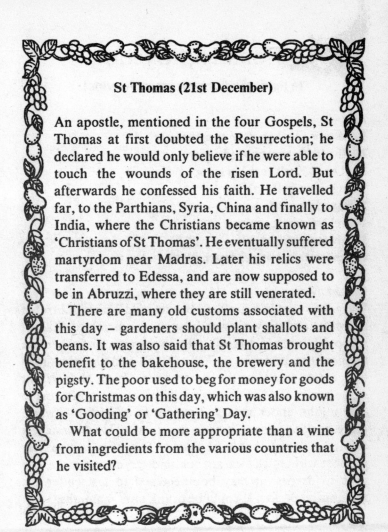

St Thomas (21st December)

An apostle, mentioned in the four Gospels, St Thomas at first doubted the Resurrection; he declared he would only believe if he were able to touch the wounds of the risen Lord. But afterwards he confessed his faith. He travelled far, to the Parthians, Syria, China and finally to India, where the Christians became known as 'Christians of St Thomas'. He eventually suffered martyrdom near Madras. Later his relics were transferred to Edessa, and are now supposed to be in Abruzzi, where they are still venerated.

There are many old customs associated with this day – gardeners should plant shallots and beans. It was also said that St Thomas brought benefit to the bakehouse, the brewery and the pigsty. The poor used to beg for money for goods for Christmas on this day, which was also known as 'Gooding' or 'Gathering' Day.

What could be more appropriate than a wine from ingredients from the various countries that he visited?

Rose Hip Syrup

(a light, medium-sweet table wine)

Ingredients
Bordeaux or all-purpose yeast starter
2¼ lb (1020g) granulated sugar
12 fl oz (340ml) rose hip syrup
2 3mg vitamin B₁ tablets
1 heaped tsp citric acid
1 level tsp pectic enzyme
1 level tsp nutrient salts
Campden tablet as per instructions

Procedure
Place the sugar in a sterilised bucket, add 2 pints (1 litre) of
hot water and stir well until the sugar has dissolved. Make it
up to 7½ pints (4.2 litres) with cold water, and when the
temperature is down to 70°F (21°C) add the remaining
ingredients, including the yeast starter. Cover, and ferment
in the bucket for 4 days, stirring daily, before transferring to
a demijohn under airlock. Ferment to a finish in a warm
place, racking as soon as the wine is stable, at which stage a
Campden tablet should be added. This wine is a general
purpose wine, but a pleasant one, and very easy to make. If it
goes to dryness it may be sweetened to taste after the
maturation period. It could be drunk after 4 months.

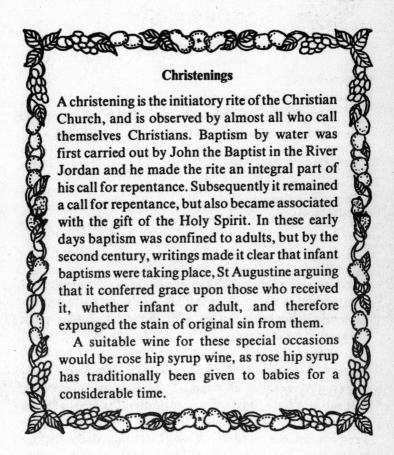

Christenings

A christening is the initiatory rite of the Christian Church, and is observed by almost all who call themselves Christians. Baptism by water was first carried out by John the Baptist in the River Jordan and he made the rite an integral part of his call for repentance. Subsequently it remained a call for repentance, but also became associated with the gift of the Holy Spirit. In these early days baptism was confined to adults, but by the second century, writings made it clear that infant baptisms were taking place, St Augustine arguing that it conferred grace upon those who received it, whether infant or adult, and therefore expunged the stain of original sin from them.

A suitable wine for these special occasions would be rose hip syrup wine, as rose hip syrup has traditionally been given to babies for a considerable time.

Rose Petal

(a light, fragrant rosé table wine)

Ingredients

Bordeaux or all-purpose yeast
starter
4 pints (2 litres) rose petals
(loosely packed)
2 lb (900g) granulated sugar
4 oz (114g) raspberries
4 oz (114g) redcurrants
Campden tablet as per
instructions

½ pint (285ml) white grape
concentrate
2 3mg vitamin B_1 tablets
1 level tsp citric acid
1 level tsp tartaric acid
1 level tsp nutrient salts
1 level tsp pectic enzyme
½ level tsp grape tannin

Procedure

Take the rose petals, which can be a blend of colours, though a few should be dark red, rinse them lightly and place them in a sterilised bucket, together with the sugar. Add 4 pints (2 litres) of tepid water, and stir until the sugar has dissolved. Wash the fruit and liquidise it in a little water (or mash it). Place it in the bucket, together with 1 Campden tablet. Cover, and leave for 24 hours. Add the grape concentrate and the remaining ingredients, including the yeast starter, and make it up to 8 pints (4.5 litres) by adding cold water. Ferment on the pulp for 4 days, stirring daily, before straining off the solids and putting the fermenting must into a demijohn under airlock. Ferment to a finish in a warm place, racking as soon as the wine is stable. This wine does not need a long maturation period, and may be drunk as a light, fresh wine within 4 or 5 months.

Weddings

A church wedding celebrates the legal and religious union of a couple. Originally marriage feasts were usually held in the house of the groom, and often at night. A steward or friend would supervise the feast, and many relatives and friends would attend, so that the wine might well run out, as at the wedding in Cana where Christ performed his first miracle. To refuse an invitation to a wedding feast was considered to be an insult.

Although champagne is the first wine that comes to mind nowadays when we think of weddings, a sparkling wine is not one that a beginner should be encouraged to make. It needs considerable care, for the pressure created in a bottle is far too great for a normal wine bottle to withstand, and it will be appreciated that if that pressure bursts a bottle, it can be very dangerous – I *never* use anything but a champagne bottle for my sparkling wines.

However, our wine for the day is derived from a very old custom associated with weddings: that of scattering rose petals on the ground before the newly wedded couple come out of the church after the ceremony. This signifies the hope that their future path will be symbolically strewn with flowers. To this day paper rose petals are used.

Sloe

(a medium-sweet social wine)

Ingredients
Burgundy or all-purpose yeast starter
3 lb (1.4kg) sloes (with stalks removed)
½ lb (227g) sultanas
3 lb (1.4 kg) granulated sugar
Campden tablets as per instructions
1 3mg vitamin B₁ tablet
1 level tsp pectic enzyme
1 level tsp nutrient salts

Procedure
Wash the sloes thoroughly. Cut or prick them and place
them in a sterilised bucket. Wash the sultanas. Liquidise
them in a little water or chop them. Add them to the bucket
with the sugar. Pour in 4 pints (2 litres) of boiling water. Stir
until the sugar has dissolved, add 1 Campden tablet, cover,
and leave overnight. After 24 hours, make it up to 8 pints
(4.5 litres) with warm water, and when the temperature is
down to 70°F (21°C) add the remaining ingredients, including the yeast starter. Ferment on the pulp for 4 days, stirring
daily, before straining the fermenting must into a demijohn
under airlock and topping up if necessary. Continue the
fermentation to completion in a warm place, racking as soon
as the wine is stable, and adding 1 Campden tablet. This wine
could be drunk after 6 months but will improve greatly with
keeping. Sweeten to taste a few days before bottling.

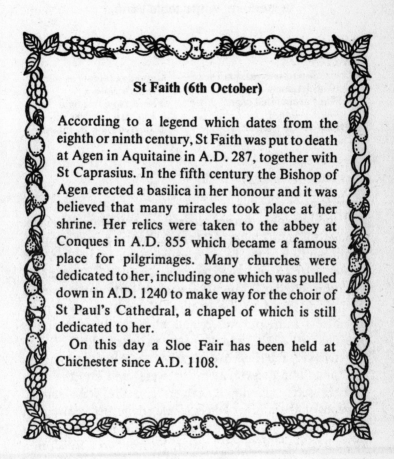

St Faith (6th October)

According to a legend which dates from the eighth or ninth century, St Faith was put to death at Agen in Aquitaine in A.D. 287, together with St Caprasius. In the fifth century the Bishop of Agen erected a basilica in her honour and it was believed that many miracles took place at her shrine. Her relics were taken to the abbey at Conques in A.D. 855 which became a famous place for pilgrimages. Many churches were dedicated to her, including one which was pulled down in A.D. 1240 to make way for the choir of St Paul's Cathedral, a chapel of which is still dedicated to her.

On this day a Sloe Fair has been held at Chichester since A.D. 1108.

173

Sultana

(a medium, white table wine)

Ingredients

Hock or all-purpose yeast starter
2 lb (900g) bananas
2 lb (900g) granulated sugar
2 lb (900g) sultanas
1 level tsp pectic enzyme

Campden tablets as per
  instructions
2 level tsp citric acid
1 level tsp nutrient salts
2 3mg vitamin B_1 tablets

Procedure

Peel the bananas, discard their skins and chop them up. Simmer them in 3 pints (1.7 litres) of water for 30 minutes. Strain, and place the liquor and the sugar into a sterilised bucket, stirring until the sugar has dissolved. Thoroughly wash the sultanas. Liquidise them in a little water or chop them. Add them to the bucket. Make it up to 6 pints (3.4 litres) with cold water, and when the temperature is down to 70°F (21°C) add the pectic enzyme and a Campden tablet, cover, and leave overnight. After 24 hours make it up to 8 pints (4.5 litres) with warm water and add the acid, nutrient salts, vitamin B_1 tablets and the yeast starter. Ferment on the pulp for 4 days, stirring daily, before straining the fermenting must into a demijohn under airlock, topping up as necessary with cold water. Ferment to a finish in a warm place, racking immediately the wine is stable, and adding 1 Campden tablet. A second racking will be necessary within 4 weeks. This wine could be drunk after 4 months.

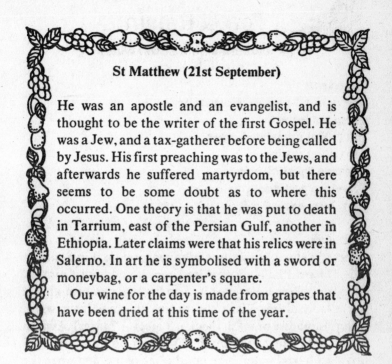

St Matthew (21st September)

He was an apostle and an evangelist, and is thought to be the writer of the first Gospel. He was a Jew, and a tax-gatherer before being called by Jesus. His first preaching was to the Jews, and afterwards he suffered martyrdom, but there seems to be some doubt as to where this occurred. One theory is that he was put to death in Tarrium, east of the Persian Gulf, another in Ethiopia. Later claims were that his relics were in Salerno. In art he is symbolised with a sword or moneybag, or a carpenter's square.

Our wine for the day is made from grapes that have been dried at this time of the year.

Tea & Raisin

(a medium-sweet social wine)

Ingredients

Sherry or all-purpose yeast starter
4 tbsp tea leaves
2 lb (900g) granulated sugar
2 lb (900g) raisins
1 heaped tsp citric acid
1 level tsp pectic enzyme
1 level tsp nutrient salts

Procedure

Select a scented Indian or China tea, and tie it in a muslin bag. Place the bag in a sterilised bucket and pour 4 pints (2 litres) of boiling water over it. Add the sugar and stir until it has all dissolved. Wash the raisins thoroughly in warm water. Liquidise or mash them in 3 pints (1.7 litres) of warm water. Add this to the bucket. Make it up to 8 pints (4.5 litres) with cold water, take out the bag of tea, and when the temperature is down to 70°F (21°C) add the remaining ingredients, including the yeast starter. Ferment for 5 days before straining into a demijohn under airlock. Ferment to a finish in a warm place, racking as soon as the wine is stable. Sweeten to taste, adding one stabilising tablet. The wine could be drunk after 3–4 months.

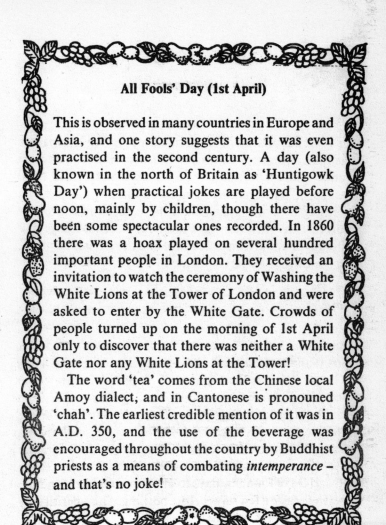

All Fools' Day (1st April)

This is observed in many countries in Europe and Asia, and one story suggests that it was even practised in the second century. A day (also known in the north of Britain as 'Huntigowk Day') when practical jokes are played before noon, mainly by children, though there have been some spectacular ones recorded. In 1860 there was a hoax played on several hundred important people in London. They received an invitation to watch the ceremony of Washing the White Lions at the Tower of London and were asked to enter by the White Gate. Crowds of people turned up on the morning of 1st April only to discover that there was neither a White Gate nor any White Lions at the Tower!

The word 'tea' comes from the Chinese local Amoy dialect, and in Cantonese is pronounced 'chah'. The earliest credible mention of it was in A.D. 350, and the use of the beverage was encouraged throughout the country by Buddhist priests as a means of combating *intemperance* – and that's no joke!

Vermouth

(a sweet aperitif)

This is an adaptation of the Grapefruit Aperitif recipe (see page 120), and we start with that finished wine. To this must be added the herbs, and the wine should be fortified to 30 proof spirit. The quantity of spirit required will depend on the strength of the grapefruit wine, and to measure this accurately we must use the Pearson Square (see page 41). Assuming that the wine is 26 proof and the spirit is 70 proof, then the ratio is 10 parts of wine to 1 part of spirit.

Procedure

Buy a packet of Vermouth herbs suitable for a sweet aperitif, and make a small cotton bag, into which the herbs can be placed. Use the quantity of herbs recommended on the packet. Tie a piece of cotton to the bag, and hang it in the demijohn (remembering to leave the cotton end outside the container) for 7–10 days (or until sufficient flavour has been extracted). Move the bag about, and shake the container daily. Remove the bag then add the spirit to the wine, shake well, and leave for a few days to allow a complete blending. Sweeten to taste a few days before bottling. This aperitif may be drunk after 4–5 months.

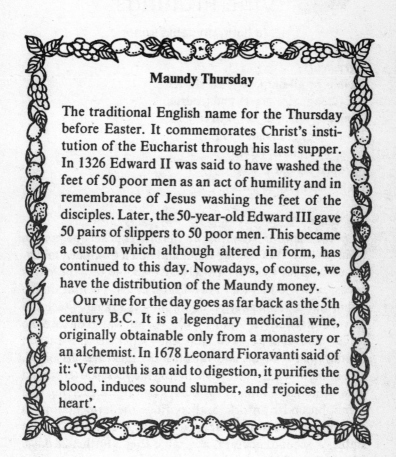

Maundy Thursday

The traditional English name for the Thursday before Easter. It commemorates Christ's institution of the Eucharist through his last supper. In 1326 Edward II was said to have washed the feet of 50 poor men as an act of humility and in remembrance of Jesus washing the feet of the disciples. Later, the 50-year-old Edward III gave 50 pairs of slippers to 50 poor men. This became a custom which although altered in form, has continued to this day. Nowadays, of course, we have the distribution of the Maundy money.

Our wine for the day goes as far back as the 5th century B.C. It is a legendary medicinal wine, originally obtainable only from a monastery or an alchemist. In 1678 Leonard Fioravanti said of it: 'Vermouth is an aid to digestion, it purifies the blood, induces sound slumber, and rejoices the heart'.

Vine Prunings

(a light, dry table wine)

Ingredients
Chablis or all-purpose yeast starter
5 lb (2.3kg) vine leaves and tendrils
Campden tablet as per instructions
3 lb (1.4kg) granulated sugar
1 3mg vitamin B$_1$ tablet
1 heaped tsp citric acid
1 level tsp nutrient salts

Procedure
Place the leaves and tendrils in a sterilised bucket and pour in 7 pints (4 litres) of boiling water and add a Campden tablet. Let is stand for 48 hours, closely covered, but turn the leaves occasionally so that they are all submerged. Then strain the liquid into a *second bucket* containing the sugar. Wash the leaves and tendrils in 1 pint ($\frac{1}{2}$ litre) of hot water, discard the leaves and tendrils and add the water to the bucket containing the sugar, and stir until the sugar has dissolved. The remaining ingredients, including the yeast starter should then be added. Ferment for 4 days before transferring to a demijohn under airlock, and continue the fermentation to completion in a warm place, racking as soon as the wine is stable. A second racking is advisable after a further 28 days. The wine could be drunk after 4 months.

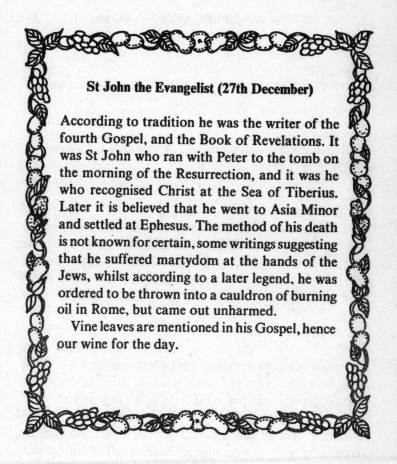

St John the Evangelist (27th December)

According to tradition he was the writer of the fourth Gospel, and the Book of Revelations. It was St John who ran with Peter to the tomb on the morning of the Resurrection, and it was he who recognised Christ at the Sea of Tiberius. Later it is believed that he went to Asia Minor and settled at Ephesus. The method of his death is not known for certain, some writings suggesting that he suffered martydom at the hands of the Jews, whilst according to a later legend, he was ordered to be thrown into a cauldron of burning oil in Rome, but came out unharmed.

Vine leaves are mentioned in his Gospel, hence our wine for the day.

Wheat & Raisin

(a medium-bodied, sweet social wine)

Ingredients

Sherry or all-purpose yeast
  starter
1 pint (½ litre) wheat
2 large potatoes
2 lb (900g) raisins
2½ lb (1.1kg) granulated sugar
2 level tsp citric acid

Campden tablets as per
  instructions
1 level tsp amylase
1 level tsp pectic enzyme
1 level tsp nutrient salts
1 3mg vitamin B_1 tablet

Procedure

Wash the wheat. Soak it overnight in 1 pt/½ litre of cold water to soften it. Next day strain off and discard the liquid. Wash (or peel if old) the potatoes and slice them. Wash the raisins well in warm water. Liquidise them and the wheat in some water or chop the raisins and bruise the wheat. Place them in a bucket. Add the sugar, potatoes, and acid, and pour over 3 pts/1.7 litres of hot (not boiling) water. Stir until the sugar has dissolved, and make it up to 8 pts/4.5 litres with cold water. Add 1 Campden tablet. Cover and leave for 24 hours. Add the amylase, pectic enzyme, nutrient salts, vitamin tablet and the yeast starter, stirring them in. Ferment in a warm place for 5 days, stirring at least once each day to break up the cap of solids which forms at the top of the fermenting must. Strain off the solids, placing the fermenting must in a demijohn under airlock. Ferment to a finish in a warm place. Rack as soon as the wine is stable and add 1 Campden tablet. This wine may be drunk after 6–9 months but will improve greatly with keeping.

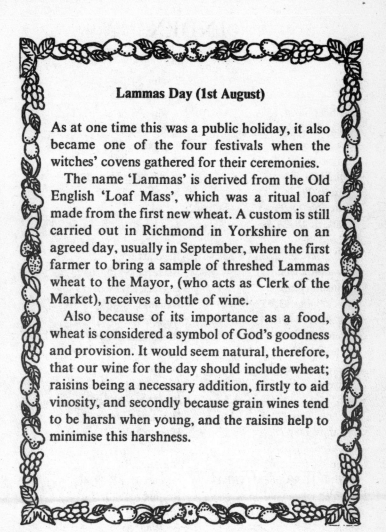

Lammas Day (1st August)

As at one time this was a public holiday, it also became one of the four festivals when the witches' covens gathered for their ceremonies.

The name 'Lammas' is derived from the Old English 'Loaf Mass', which was a ritual loaf made from the first new wheat. A custom is still carried out in Richmond in Yorkshire on an agreed day, usually in September, when the first farmer to bring a sample of threshed Lammas wheat to the Mayor, (who acts as Clerk of the Market), receives a bottle of wine.

Also because of its importance as a food, wheat is considered a symbol of God's goodness and provision. It would seem natural, therefore, that our wine for the day should include wheat; raisins being a necessary addition, firstly to aid vinosity, and secondly because grain wines tend to be harsh when young, and the raisins help to minimise this harshness.

INDEX

RIGHT WAY
PUBLISHING POLICY

HOW WE SELECT TITLES
RIGHT WAY consider carefully every deserving manuscript. Where an author is an authority on his subject but an inexperienced writer, we provide first-class editorial help. The standards we set make sure that every **RIGHT WAY** book is practical, easy to understand, concise, informative and delightful to read. Our specialist artists are skilled at creating simple illustrations which augment the text wherever necessary.

CONSISTENT QUALITY
At every reprint our books are updated where appropriate, giving our authors the opportunity to include new information.

FAST DELIVERY
We sell **RIGHT WAY** books to the best bookshops throughout the world. It may be that your bookseller has run out of stock of a particular title. If so, he can order more from us at any time – we have a fine reputation for "same day" despatch, and we supply any order, however small (even a single copy), to any bookseller who has an account with us. We prefer you to buy from your bookseller, as this reminds him of the strong underlying public demand for **RIGHT WAY** books. Readers who live in remote places, or who are housebound, or whose local bookseller is unco-operative, can order direct from us by post.

FREE
If you would like an up-to-date list of all **RIGHT WAY** titles currently available, send a stamped self-addressed envelope to
ELLIOT RIGHT WAY BOOKS,
LOWER KINGSWOOD, TADWORTH, SURREY,
KT20 6TD,U.K.
or visit our web site at www.right-way.co.uk